IF ONLY GOD WOULD ANSWER

What to Do When You Ask, Seek, and Knock—and Nothing Happens

STEVEN MOSLEY

NAVPRESS

BRINGING TRUTH TO LIFE
NavPress Publishing Group
P.O. Box 35001, Colorado Springs, Colorado 80935

The Navigators is an international Christian organization. Jesus Christ gave His followers the Great Commission to go and make disciples (Matthew 28:19). The aim of The Navigators is to help fulfill that commission by multiplying laborers for Christ in every nation.

NavPress is the publishing ministry of The Navigators. NavPress publications are tools to help Christians grow. Although publications alone cannot make disciples or change lives, they can help believers learn biblical discipleship, and apply what they learn to their lives and ministries.

Library of Congress Catalog Card Number: 92-62811
ISBN 08910-97120

Cover illustration: Roberta Polfus
Interior illustrations: Craig Simmons

Unless otherwise identified, all Scripture in this publication is from the *Holy Bible: New International Version* (NIV). Copyright © 1973, 1978, 1984, International Bible Society. Used by permission of Zondervan Bible Publishers. Other versions used include: the *New American Standard Bible* (NASB), © The Lockman Foundation 1960, 1962, 1963, 1968, 1971, 1972, 1973, 1975, 1977; and the *Amplified New Testament* (AMP), © The Lockman Foundation 1954, 1958.

Printed in the United States of America

Contents

*To my friends
in Campus Crusade for Christ
who turned prayer into a movement*

PART ONE

Making Our Prayers More Answerable

Everyone always tells you to be specific in prayer. If you don't ask, you won't get, they say. But sometimes when you're most specific, agonizingly specific, you seem to head straight into a brick wall. The malignant tumor steadily draining your loved one of strength is horribly particular; the pink slip that arrived so unexpectedly on your desk was painfully particular; those drugs you found under your teenager's bed were shockingly particular. You've prayed long and hard about these specific problems; you've been asking for God's intervention—but the heavens seem indifferent. You've made careful requests night after night on your knees until your eyes are red and blurry. Yet, nothing seems to happen.

You hear other people's stories of dramatic answers to prayer, and you wonder, "What about me?" You see all the assurances, all the promises in the Bible, and you wonder, "What about me? How did I miss out?"

I am haunted by the faces of those who've been disappointed in prayer.

I remember the tall, big-boned physical therapist who usually found some way to talk about Christ with his patients.

One day this active believer shared, in his amiable, quiet way, a private tragedy: "I just don't have much success with prayer. God doesn't seem to answer mine."

I also remember intense, distinguished-looking Joseph too, an earnest Christian who'd experienced several keen disappointments. Whenever the family devotional book had a story that involved a dramatic answer to prayer, he invariably cautioned his kids: "This doesn't mean God is in the habit of answering prayer like that." Sometimes he sounded like a broken record, but he wanted to protect his children from disappointment. Pray, yes, by all means. But just don't count on it.

What happens to people who've been disappointed in prayer? Some grow bitter. Others place their faith on hold. Most struggle on in the Christian life, a little lonelier, a little less sure. The phrase "Thy will be done" turns into resignation.

I get the feeling that many of us keep missing the target and so, finally, decide simply to remove it. We determine that prayer isn't about getting answers. It's about changing me, or submitting to God.

But is that all there is?

Just how should we as believers relate to the petition part of prayer? Is there anything we can count on? Is there a way to make our prayers more answerable?

In this book you'll find specific answers to the questions that cause real perplexity and heartache. I want to show you the tools that turn prayer into something consistently joyful and rewarding. Above all, I want to show you how healthy petition can immeasurably enrich your relationship with God. In part 1 we'll begin that step-by-step process, working from problems to doable solutions. Part 2 will solidify your experiment with answerable prayer by untying a few final knots that sometimes paralyze petition.

It's my belief that prayer is much less a shot in the dark than many of us have reluctantly concluded. Regularly answered prayer is the birthright of every believer, not just the gift of a few high-flying saints. Scripture indicates there are specific things we can do to make our prayers more effective. We can develop skill in prayer with a little careful attention and the right kind of practice.

Why can't I have a beautiful garden like my neighbor's?

God's answer is closer than you think.

CHAPTER ONE

Step by Step

TIM AND YOLAND began their romance quite precariously, and it got worse as they went along. I remember seeing them in the evening, outside the school where Tim and I worked, carrying on intricate arguments in the dark, their gestures a mixture of pleading and accusation. They rushed into marriage anyway. Their emotional instability and unresolved conflict trailed after them like noisy tin cans tied to a car, headed off to the honeymoon.

Several years and two children later, Tim and Yoland settled down in a community not far from where my wife, Kaz, and I were raising our kids. Yoland began to pour out her sorrows on my sympathetic wife. They were considerable. Tim treated her like dirt—whenever he happened to show up at the house. He'd turned his back on God and grimly set about to pursue the pleasures of the world: other women. At one time he'd moved in with one.

Kaz tried to help Yoland build up her self-esteem, but Tim's erratic behavior kept her on an emotional roller coaster. He was fairly considerate as a father; their two sons loved him. And on those occasions when he'd show a little kindness to Yoland, she'd fervently hope and pray that things were changing. But then, Tim would become verbally abusive again and head off to his girlfriend.

Tragically, though Yoland found her marriage unendurable, the alternative of living alone seemed even worse. She constantly sobbed out her stories of yet another cruel disappointment, but she could not bring herself to divorce this man. Yoland believed that there would not be another.

So she kept flailing her prayers against this no-win situation, begging God to change her husband. If only Tim's heart were touched somehow, everything would be different; they would have a home again. She prayed and hoped—and was crushed—year after year.

Many people, like Yoland, find their prayer life locked on an intractable problem. No solutions are in sight; only a miracle can change things. So they desperately keep butting their petitions against the obstacle.

Let's look at an alternative to this kind of frustration. First an important principle: Our prayers about such problems often run into a brick wall because we tend to focus exclusively on the final, complete solution. That is, we only pray about the long-term, end result, not *the means* to that end. We may aim specifically, but we're pointing a long way off.

We want Uncle Charlie, who shows no interest in religion, to become a born-again believer.

We want the family in which constant fighting between Mom and Dad is emotionally maiming the children to become a model Christian home.

We want the loved one dying of cancer to rebound to perfect health.

We want the addict to lose all desire for that pernicious drug.

We want the compulsive adulterer to return to his spouse and kids.

These goals are certainly commendable. But we must recognize that they aim at the end of the road. It will help immensely if we break our requests down into smaller, shorter-term petitions. Dramatic events are usually the accumulated result of many smaller occurrences. It helps to focus on the first thing that needs to happen. What is the initial step toward that distant goal?

Let's take the unbelieving, uninterested relative. What would move him from square one to square two? An awareness of some spiritual value? Admiration for the beauty God created in nature? Think about Uncle Charlie and his interests, then pray about what would be his most likely first step toward God. Then think about the means of encouraging that initial response. Is there a book that might interest him? A person he could meet?

Too often religious thinking follows a black or white, all or nothing, pattern. Agnostic Charlie is dwelling in utter darkness and must make a quantum leap to the light where his actions and beliefs will all be pure. We don't think much about the progression from one to the other.

God's Spirit is certainly capable of transforming people dramatically. But most of us take long, meandering walks into the light. Even when a miraculous encounter with God does occur, people have usually taken quite a few steps to get to that point.

"Established" Christians, however, may find it hard to affirm anything less than "the truth, the whole truth, and nothing but the truth." We feel we compromise the faith if we commend belief or behavior that's not quite up to standard. And so we're not very good at nurturing those hesitant, awkward first steps of faith. In fact, sometimes our zealous rigidity in seeking that complete transformation becomes an obstacle in the way of those groping toward God. They see no way to ever reach our lofty goal. Why even begin?

Vague talk about God as a Spirit may appear a pathetic watering down of biblical truth to the orthodox believer, but it could be a great revelation for someone who's never before given the Almighty a thought. We may criticize parents who watch television at home every night, but that may indicate real progress for those who used to leave the kids to go out drinking.

What about people like Tim, the husband caught in chronic adultery? Of course we want him back home with his wife and kids, as a godly husband and father. But what's the first nudge that can get him off his present track? What could happen to him to suggest how infinitely valuable his family is?

Kaz and I tried to get Yoland focused on her own next step: How could she start to grow in this situation? We encouraged her to aim more of her prayers at God's love and acceptance, establishing a consistent devotional life. Only as she became emotionally stronger could she have a significant influence over her husband. In some ways Yoland had become an enabler of Tim's unfaithfulness by keeping her home and heart open to him—in the same way that the families of problem drinkers become co-alcoholics by cleaning up after them and carrying them home and making excuses for them at work.

By aiming at her own first steps forward, at immediate goals, Yoland could experience a much healthier and more answerable prayer life. Kaz and I noticed that when she responded and got serious about her own relationship with God, her emotional roller coaster did even out; she wasn't quite so vulnerable. Small steps, yes. The miracle hasn't happened yet. But the important thing is that Yoland is walking instead of just waiting.

▼

SOLUTION CENTERED

When I first descended toward Osaka, the red and white stream of traffic on the dark plain below stretched beyond even the broad horizon we could see from our DC-10. Several times I thought we'd come to the end. Surely there couldn't be any more—at this speed. But as we flew on and on, the lighted buildings beneath formed an endless constellation.

Later, riding from the airport to our apartments, I stared at the gray nondescript buildings—like any city's, I guessed.

But I imagined all the people who must live and move and have their being in that place. I was supposed to be a missionary there and help spread the good word. But somehow this target metropolis seemed very depressing; I felt rather helpless.

That first impression deepened the following day while rushing through train stations on the way to the English school where I would teach. All the people flooded by with blank commuter faces. Trains disgorged multitudes every minute into the sea of dark business suits, dark eyes, dark hair. I wondered how many of those eyes ever glanced heavenward.

My prayers those first few nights in Japan seemed terribly frail in the face of this overwhelming problem: a deeply secular culture effortlessly drowning out our squeaky little words about God.

Then I got into my first Bible class and our forbidding environment suddenly changed. I wasn't dealing with "the Japanese people" anymore; I was introducing myself to six human beings with faces and names and varying degrees of interest in the gospel. My initial efforts at communicating my faith were certainly awkward and experimental, but they were steps toward Junko and Kioji and Kenji.

Now my petitions could take good aim. I could pray about those students and their questions and what might turn on the next light for them. I didn't feel as overwhelmed or powerless any more.

When I looked at the great task of evangelizing Japan, I could think only of enormous difficulties, and my prayer remained a nervous gesture in the dark. But when that long-term goal was broken down into six people today, I started to think and pray in terms of solutions: how to reach Junko; what to say to Kioji. I was looking at the steps and not just at the end of the road.

Concentrating on steps helps us to become solution-centered as opposed to problem-centered. When we just throw out a shotgun prayer at some big problem, it remains a big problem. When we break it down into component parts and pray about the first one, we naturally begin to focus on specific remedies.

God is evidently a solution-centered Being—even though He could have no end of things to moan about in regard to life on this planet. The whole Bible could easily have been one long, divine gripe session: There they go again . . . stealing, raping, fighting. But God's Word, all of it, builds to one climax: the coming of Jesus Christ and God's ultimate solution on Golgotha. All the epistles explain and amplify and glorify that solution. The Apostle Paul, the preeminent church builder who faced all kinds of problems in various congregations, couldn't stop writing about the solution. It spills out everywhere in his letters, no matter what topic he's discussing.

So, if God is solution-centered, petitioning Him in a solution-centered manner makes sense. We're more on His wavelength that way, and it's a much healthier wavelength to begin with. We aim more at where we want to go than at what we want to avoid. God desires to reinforce healthy attitudes and discourage negative, obsessive ones. That's something to think about the next time you address some chronic misfortune.

One morning while I was attempting to make granola in the kitchen, one of my fellow-teachers at the school shuffled in, sank down on a chair, and hesitantly began to share her despair. Sonya was the new kid in Japan, full of a wide-eyed innocence I thought had been eradicated from the earth. I had noticed her the first day of school, trembling in the hallway and taking a deep breath before entering the English class she taught. Now her vulnerability extended openly across her face. Anyone else sitting there so pale and doe-eyed, staring down at Little Orphan Annie hands, would have to be faking it. But I knew this girl's frailty went to the bone.

Sonya said she didn't think she could ever be a missionary. The task of trying to communicate the gospel to people for whom God was a mystifying stranger had overwhelmed her. Most of us had experienced quite a jolt when we realized that the Christian clichés we'd grown up with were falling on deaf ears. Our students hadn't a clue as to what all these wonderful expressions meant. We had to do some serious digging, both in the Bible and in our own lives.

For Sonya this proved devastating. She didn't think she knew Christ herself.

So there we sat in the kitchen, with soggy gray lumps of would-be granola all over the table. Sonya had enough difficulty just relating to her peers, how could she function as a missionary teacher before skeptical young professionals? There seemed no way to get there from here.

Knowing how to pray was difficult when staring at this formidable problem. But fortunately I had recently become excited about a certain method of devotional Bible study. It presented itself as a first step, and we began to look at a solution.

If Sonya could just experience God teaching her, speaking to her individually, if she could just get a few insights from the Word, maybe she could become a teacher to others. We talked a long time. Sonya ended up agreeing to try to develop a meaningful quiet time and promised to start writing down what she learned each day.

I began praying that God would make His Word come alive in her hands, sparking revelations, creating new abilities. After a few days Sonya shared something exciting she'd seen in Jesus' forgiveness of the woman caught in adultery. I thought her cheeks rosier than usual. Her eyes flickered a bit.

Sonya kept learning and sharing—morning by morning, step by step. Soon she was helping a few Japanese friends who had hang-ups about the church. She was taking off. Her devotional life blossomed, and she began wielding God's Word in Bible classes to great effect.

Then her emotionally disturbed sister flew in for a visit. Their relationship had been difficult because of trauma in their childhood home (the principal reason for Sonya's vulnerability). Now Sonya became the healer. She could reach out, instead of just trying to protect herself. As she shared what she'd been learning, her sister saw the good news as if for the first time and told Sonya: "I want what you guys have." Little Orphan Annie had struck it rich.

The Coach Potato
School of Prayer

CHAPTER TWO

Setting Up a Rendezvous

WHEN JAMES RELAXED in the evening after a long day at the office, he did so with a kind of sovereign immobility. He would plop down with a great sigh into his comfortable chair in the den, glance at the paper, and then begin calling out requests. His kids fetched his slippers, closed the windows, tossed him the *TV Guide*, brought ice water, put the dog out, brought pop and potato chips, let the dog in, brought donuts, turned on the heater, brought a platter of cold cuts.

It wasn't that the children were worked so hard; James had developed asking for things into a fine art and stretched out these requests over the whole evening. It was always "While you're up . . ." and "When you get a chance. . . ." He directed the proceedings with such good cheer and skill that guests rarely noticed he never moved from his recliner.

My picture of my friend James would not be at all unpleasant, except for one fact: his considerable obesity. The man could break into a sweat walking down the hall to the bathroom. He desperately needed exercise, but his sprightly, healthy kids were the ones who bounced around all evening, responding to Dad's repeated pleas—for peanuts or onion dip or popcorn.

Sometimes we can fall into a spiritual type of obesity in our prayer life. We get in the habit of tossing requests up to God for all kinds of things (after all, our Father urges us to ask) without realizing that part of God's answer may include our getting up from the couch. That's easy to forget in a world full of laborsaving devices and remote controls, where more and more things happen as we do less and less.

It surprised me to learn recently that many of the angelic messages recorded in the Bible could be summarized in two words: "Hurry up!" Typically, when we think of angels wafting down in a pool of light to speak to mere mortals, we assume that a soothing greeting-card axiom will follow. But their voices are actually closer to an alarm clock at seven a.m.

An angel bursts in on Peter, chained in a dungeon, and calls out, "Rise quickly." Gideon stops his wheat threshing at Ophrah to hear the angel of the Lord say, "Arise and go in this thy might." A despairing Elijah hears the command, "Get up and eat." When Herod is slaughtering the innocents an angel wakes up Joseph with the words, "Go quickly." Another heavenly messenger sets Philip off in pursuit of the Ethiopian eunich with, "Arise and go."[1]

Clearly angels who come in answer to prayer don't leave us sitting for long. Part of the secret of answerable prayer is what we do after we pray. We'll never experience the joy of great answers as long as we spend most of our time on the couch, sending occasional petitions like remote control signals and waiting for some act of providence to show up like an entertaining TV show. Miracles are a participant phenomenon; they rarely happen to bystanders. If we're waiting for God to perform for us as we relax in the pew or living room, we'll witness very little.

Jacques Ellul warned about "disincarnate prayers," which substitute good private feelings for actions and justify noninvolvement. He pointed out that when the disciples were pondering the problem of a hungry multitude,

Jesus told them, "*You* give them something to eat." In writing about the same problem, C. S. Lewis observed, "It's so much easier to pray for a bore than to go and see him." Lewis concluded that the kind of faith that can receive whatever it asks "occurs only when the one who prays does so as God's fellow-worker, demanding what is needed for the joint work . . . the colleague of God is so united with Him at certain moments that something of the divine foreknowledge enters his mind."[2]

GOD IN THE THICK OF IT

Prayer is most answerable when it seizes on divine initiatives, reaching out to meet needs with divine resources. This is one key factor distinguishing those whose prayers seem to trigger acts of providence from those whose prayers seem to trickle away without a trace. The former tend to be active, seeking to carry out God's purposes by His means. The latter tend to be passive, reacting to things that threaten their comfort or security.

Why do all those great stories of miraculous answers to prayer come from African jungle villages or obscure Chinese provinces? Why does it appear that God is visibly active only in the mission field? A skeptic may assume that providential drama gets added as the stories are passed along from hinterland to American Sunday school. A bigger reason, I think, is that God is most active when we are reaching out most. He stretches out when we stretch out.

Think about the classic examples. Why did George Müller report a book full of answers to specific prayer in complacent Victorian England? He was seeking to meet the needs of two thousand orphans. Why could Hudson Taylor in remotest China report such inspiring experiences about receiving just the funds or personnel needed without ever making an appeal to any human being? He was stretching out to share the gospel where it had not been shared before. Why did God's Smuggler, Brother Andrew, have such an abundance of dramatic responses to his petitions? He was given completely to a mission: taking Bibles behind the iron curtain. God is most active in the thick of it.

George Whitefield met his fiercest opposition and witnessed the most dramatic conversions while preaching in the open air at a London fairgrounds full of strolling players, bear baiters, merry-andrews, pickpockets, and gin sellers. When Whitefield drew large crowds around his makeshift platform, he aroused the ire of the secular showmen. They tried mocking him and then shouting him down—both without success. Then they picked up a huge maypole and charged the outer edge of the crowd. This battering ram was dangerous: bones could break; men and women could die in the crush to get away. Eyes flickered in terror.

Whitefield paused in his sermon, shouted a warning to the crowd, and began to pray aloud, asking the Lord of hosts to intervene. Suddenly the group of rowdies running with their cumbersome projectile began yelling and gesturing at each other. A dispute erupted. They dropped the maypole and began flailing away at each other. Finally the leaders slunk off. Some of the men, however, decided to stay, and a few were actually converted.[3]

George Whitefield, like many others, saw God respond dramatically to prayer because he stepped into the drama.

▼

ACTIVE PRAYER

In a time when the French upper class considered extramarital affairs to be an important art form, a certain noblewoman decided to turn this practice on its head. She slipped a discreet note to an attractive gentleman she was fond of and asked him to meet her on a certain street corner in Paris at midnight. Both of them made arrangements to be "unattached" that night. The woman quietly ordered her finest carriage readied, got herself dressed to kill, and proceeded to the rendezvous.

God amplifies prayful action.

She found the dashing gentleman waiting at the right spot. He quickly jumped into the carriage and swept his beloved into his arms. Then the two, husband and wife, proceeded on to enjoy the evening together.

This noblewoman found a way to inject all the electricity of a secret tryst with a lover into what her contemporaries regarded as the most uninteresting of relationships. The couple carried on this "affair" for much of their married life.

Those of us who've sunk into a rather dull, passive prayer life that remotes up requests to God from the comfort of our living room, need to catch some of that electricity. We need to put a little adventure into our relationship with Christ.

I've found that God's providences multiply as soon as I take a step of faith. Inertia is among the biggest problems we face in the spiritual life. You have to expend a little energy in order to receive divine energy. You have to be mobile in order to be moved toward the miraculous. Passive prayer is a long shot: It hopes to snag that rare occasion when God simply bursts out of the blue and overturns events single-handedly. Active prayer is much more of a sure thing; it's aimed at God acting through us, something He has expressed an intense interest in doing.

Let's give active prayer a functional definition: *setting up a rendezvous with God.* Here's how it works. First you see a need: your spouse is depressed; your child's schoolmate is neglected by his parents; a neighbor is too busy for church; a coworker is wilting under job pressure. Think and pray: How can God meet that need? What does He want to do for this person? Then formulate a petition in which you cooperate with God in meeting that need. Don't just send God out by remote control—"Go and help her, Lord." *You* find a way to get involved. You set up a rendezvous, asking to meet the Lord and His resources at the point of that need. Prayerfully decide to talk to the neighbor, friend, or spouse, at this place, that time. Ask God to arrange the right circumstances, enable you to be of assistance, and make something good happen. Now you're in the drama, not on the sidelines, and you will begin to see God act graciously through you.

Setting up a rendezvous avoids two opposite mistakes. You don't go out there alone, trying to play the part of the rescuer; but neither do you camp on the sofa and expect God to act at your command. You go out to meet God and cooperate with what He is doing for the person.

The more careful your aim the better the results. The more definite your rendezvous the better. Vague petitions about being of "some help" to so-and-so tend to get vague answers. But thinking and praying and listening enough to see a specific need and a specific way to meet that need will result in much more answerable petitions.

Obscure Chinese provinces and African villages don't have a lock on God's dramatic intervention. He is active wherever people are reaching out. He can be active in your town, your street, your house—if you will just get off the sofa and set up a rendezvous. You may not see angels swooping down from the heavens or conversions tick off like clockwork, but things will happen to give you an exciting sense that, yes, God was with you, He set up something, there *was* a rendezvous.

I'll never forget the first time I caught a sense of this kind of providential meeting. It was early in the morning, I was staring out my window at a gnarled tree and felt moved to pray for something to happen, really happen. I'd just read verses in one of Paul's epistles on encouragement and building up one another. Tired of generic resolves to be nice, of sliding through days without observable ripple, I felt an urge to take God from my devotions out into the next sixteen waking hours.

Somewhere, surely, there must be a specific rendezvous with His will. So I said, "Lord, lead me to someone I can really help today." It was not your everyday nod toward goodness. I wanted to be aimed at a target.

I went through my morning English classes as usual at the school where I taught and then we had our staff meeting.

Afterward a teacher named Peggy stopped me in the hallway. "I need to talk to you," she said with unsettling directness. "Can we go somewhere?"

We went to an unoccupied classroom. And there she spilled the beans. Peggy felt like a fake, didn't know why she was there as a missionary. She unleashed a flood of insecurity and inadequacy, hinting that her family life had been raw on the edges. The English teacher dissolved into a hurting, fearful child.

She'd been perceived by the rest of us as a loud, graceless type—not the easiest to like. Now I saw deeper.

Nothing like this had ever happened to me before. I had not been much of a listener or shoulder to cry on—just the old male cliché: quiet, self-sufficient, content with work and an occasional game of football.

Now I was so excited about having reached that rendezvous with the person God wanted me to help, I became all ears. I tried to understand weakness. And I managed to offer a few suggestions on how to acquire a stable spiritual life.

With time, other earfuls would follow from other rendezvous (like the one with Sonya), because in that providential meeting God's eagerness to serve became contagious. I sensed it sharply. He wanted me out there with Him, touching people with His hand, speaking with His words, helping to sweep others into His arms of grace.

Our prayer life must be more than
a passive reaction to disaster.

CHAPTER THREE

Defense Versus Offense

TERRY AND VIVIAN had been living out of their car for weeks when my friend Martin invited them to stay in his home. After a while he brought the young couple to church and introduced them. They seemed bright and talented. Terry was gifted musically and had been trying to produce some songs. Several in the congregation were eager to help—you don't meet too many homeless people in our suburb.

Martin arranged for job interviews. I let them use an older car for transportation. Things improved and then . . . they sort of disappeared. Once in a while one of us might run into Vivian at the mall where she worked and say hi. But for some reason it was always hard to talk, hard to know how they were really doing.

Then much later Martin got a phone call. Vivian was frantic; Terry had quit his job again to go off in pursuit of a long-shot music contract. They were out of money. Martin rushed to intervene.

The pattern continued. We were able to make contact with the couple only in their moments of desperation. Eventually it became apparent that they had never absorbed basic habits of financial thrift and perseverance.

We knew that their upbringing had been rather chaotic and still wanted to help. We wanted, above all, to establish some kind of relationship so that we could help them learn principles that might solve their chronic problems. But they were extremely difficult to contact. We saw them only when they came knocking with a look of panic on their faces.

If we take an honest look at our prayer life as a whole, we may find something similar to the situation with Terry and Vivian. We come to God earnestly and remain long in His presence only when emergencies strike. In praying for other people, as we noted in the last chapter, it's usually the Couch Potato School of Prayer that trips us up. But in praying for ourselves, a focus on disaster often decreases the effectiveness of petition.

That tendency is quite understandable from a human point of view. Prayer is typically seen as a last recourse, something most appropriate when we're overwhelmed. We do what we can in life, then, when we come to the end of our rope, ask for divine intervention. When all else fails, pray.

It would be sad to end up like the irreligious sailor who, as his ship was tossed about in the sea, cried out, "O Lord, I have not asked You for anything for fifteen years, and if You deliver us out of this storm, I promise I will not bother You for another fifteen years."

Our prayer life needs to be something more than a defensive reaction to misfortune. The problem is, when things are going okay we tend to pray vaguely, when things go bad we pray specifically. Too often we're moved to entreat earnestly only when all hell is breaking loose. As long as our family is reasonably intact and our livelihood fairly secure, we send up only standby, generic requests.

A good question to ask yourself is this: Do my prayers, as a whole, tend to make me more active or more passive? If we cry to God only when the deck is stacked against us, we will always plead while falling backward. If we employ pointed petition only in emergencies, we greatly restrict its capacity to prevail in the world.

It's a good idea, of course, to pray when calamity strikes. Yes, we should call on God when totally flattened by misfortune; yes, we may turn to prayer when all else has failed. The problem comes when we allow disasters to dominate our petitions, when dropping on our knees becomes primarily a way to dodge some blow. There are important reasons why this is a poor substitute for answerable prayer and why it tends to limit rather than expand God's area of influence in our lives.

MANY DISASTERS ARE PREVENTABLE

Our heavenly Father greatly prefers the field of preventive medicine to traumatic surgery. That is, He would like to become active in our lives long before all hell breaks loose; He would rather build us up than patch us up.

Take financial disasters, for example. A great many of them result from poor planning or just plain irresponsible spending. If God comes to the rescue every time we go broke, then He reinforces our tendency to blow cash at the wrong time for the wrong things. No good parent wants to subsidize his child's irresponsibility.

Then consider family disasters: a father abandons his family or a teenager drops out into the drug world. A great many big and little decisions led up to these traumatic events. Families generally unravel in bits and pieces. If we turn to God in earnest only when things fall apart, then we give Him an exceedingly restricted space in which to work. People may hope that God will suddenly reverse the flow of their lives with a magic wand, but He usually does not impose His goodwill on a long string of poor human choices.

Even disastrous physical afflictions are sometimes preventable. We are not dying from many contagious diseases these days; epidemics don't wipe us out. We're dying from chronic illness. Cancer and heart disease and a host of other current killers are related to choices in our diet and lifestyle.

These diseases are often preventable. If we abuse our bodies for decades and then, when our organs go on strike, plead for healing, we give God very little room in which to respond. Answering us miraculously means, in effect, reinforcing our bad health habits. Certainly God can and does heal the undeserving. None of us can claim assistance on the basis of a perfect record. But how much better to aim our prayers before we are wheeled into the operating room, before the options constrict dramatically.

If you want to make your petitions much more answerable, start concentrating on the prevention side of disaster.

▼

THE VALUE OF TROUBLE

Ioannis Metaxas, the general who ruled Greece in the 1930s, was once invited to test a new "flying boat" at an air base. He took the aircraft up for a short flight and was coming in for a landing when the base commander sitting beside him intervened politely: "Excuse me, General. It would be better to come down on the water. This is a flying boat."

Metaxas, who was about to drop the wheelless plane on a runway, quickly gunned it upward and circled around toward the water. He maneuvered the flying boat down nicely and skied to a stop. Switching off the engine, the General turned to his host and said, "Thank you, Commander, for preventing me from making a stupid blunder." With those words he briskly opened the aircraft's door, hopped out, and sank into the water.

It's nice to be rescued from major disasters, but unfortunate if we still haven't quite got the point after it's over. Several New Testament passages tell us that God is eager for us to learn from our trials. He wants us to come out of these experiences as different people—and not sink in over our heads as soon as we reach what we assume is solid ground.

The Apostle James actually tells us to consider it "joy" when trials come our way for "the testing of [our] faith" (1:2).

Lord–just for a few minutes–can't you remove my little
"thorn-in-the-flesh"?

Have you listened to
your trials lately?

We must conclude that affliction is one important tool God employs to help us grow. So if our loudest and longest cries to Him are that He drop the instrument as quickly as possible, then, again, we simply restrict His sphere of influence in our lives.

When we begin to take careful aim in prayer, it's best to aim at what God has expressed an interest in doing the most. That is, aim for the center of the target first. What does God promise most? What does He declare Himself eager to do?

Let's look at the context of some of Christ's most flagrant guarantees regarding prayer. Within Jesus' farewell discourses to the disciples, recorded in John 14–16, we find several of His most quoted promises: I will give "whatever you ask in my name"; "ask whatever you wish"; I'll do "whatever you ask." If we examine the themes that surround these extravagant statements we find that Jesus is talking about the Son bringing glory to the Father, about the Comforter coming to minister to us, about abiding in the Vine and bearing much fruit.

All this relates to spiritual growth, to accomplishing things that bring glory to God. We may pray about anything of course, but if we want to maximize the effectiveness of our prayers it makes sense to aim most frequently at what God is most eager to do. So it's best to make spiritual growth the core element of petition.

Still, this idea of trials "testing our faith" has tripped up a lot of people. The aphorism that God sends trials in order to "test" us is perhaps unfortunate. It suggests that our heavenly Father can't quite figure out where we are spiritually, so He must send a calamity to see if we pass muster, measuring our response like a physician checking a patient's heartbeat on a treadmill.

God doesn't need to test anyone in this sense. He knows what's happening inside us better than we do ourselves. The testing the Bible talks about is related to iron ore "tested" in a furnace. Peter encourages the suffering with the thought that their faith is being refined by fire, like gold (1 Peter 1:7). The dross is burned away and pure gold emerges. This "testing" is carried out in order that something good can happen, in order that the material will be transformed. The experience is for our benefit, not for God's.

Our Lord can use bad events to good effect: refining qualities like perseverance, maturity, and wisdom—traits that James mentions in the passage about the value of tribulation. But we must be careful here. This is not the same as saying that God creates misfortune to bring about growth. Disasters occur primarily because of the fundamental disaster of sin. Our planet in rebellion has separated itself from God and, therefore, lurches along out of whack to a great extent. Nature groans under the curse of humankind's moral fall. So trials are part of the chaos of life in a sinful world. As such, they often strike at random and usually seem terribly unjust. No one can make a case that misfortune is apportioned out equally to all human beings.

Consider those people who seem to get more than their share of afflictions. If they believe that God Himself is manufacturing these disasters for their spiritual benefit, they will have a hard time praising or loving Him. They'll wonder, "Why do I have to grow so much? How about that moral slob over there who's gliding along on easy street, doesn't he deserve a few calamities to wake him up?"

Disasters happen because sin happened. God is not the origin of evil. As James put it: God does not tempt anyone. We are not promised a fair and just existence on this planet. In fact we are guaranteed that some undeserved suffering will come our way. But God does promise this: "Nothing can possibly happen to you that I cannot use to benefit you in some way. I work for your good in all things."

So how should you pray? Look for that beneficial side effect of your misfortune that God is working to bring about. You may certainly ask to be rescued and plead for the affliction to be removed. That may be God's will. But keep your primary focus on spiritual growth. Ask God to show you what you can learn from this experience. Pointing persistently toward that target ensures that you'll hit something.

▼

PRAYERS ON OFFENSE

At the beginning of his ministry, Josh McDowell helped organize Christian outreach on college campuses in South America. On one occasion he helped arrange for a series of evangelistic meetings that showed great promise. A large, attentive crowd appeared on the first night. But others in town were deeply prejudiced against the "evangelicos." As the singing began, a man on an extremely loud motorcycle started racing back and forth on the street in front of the auditorium. People could hardly hear what was going on.

Josh and his associates gathered in a back room and decided to call on their "position in Christ" as believers. They claimed in prayer the fact that they had been co-resurrected, co-ascended and co-seated with Christ at the right hand of God, as described in Ephesians 2. These men claimed authority (on the basis of Christ's gracious act) to silence this opposition, right then.

Shortly after they'd risen from their knees, the piercing whine of the motorcycle's engine suddenly climaxed in an explosion. Josh ran outside and found the rider picking himself up from the asphalt and staring at a prostrated machine. The engine had completely blown and left the motorcycle a wreck. As they gathered around the man, the "evangelicos" were quite solicitous and helped him get a truck to take his bike to a shop. Then they went back inside and had a wonderful meeting.

The picture of prayer that stands out in the New Testament is of people on the offense, people moving forward. Believers are urged to come boldly before God's throne of grace, making petitions about everything on all occasions with all kinds of prayers.

New Testament prayer
turns disasters upside down.

In the epistles, prayer requests are most often linked to the rapid spread of the gospel and the advance of Christ's Kingdom. Christians are encouraged to seek wisdom and revelation, perseverance and power. Intercessors are said to wrestle in prayer for the spiritual growth and maturity of others.[1] In the New Testament, petition comes across as a dynamic agent of change, something that seizes the initiative and seeks to accomplish a specific good. It goes on the offensive; it outmaneuvers the forces of evil; it doesn't just react to disaster. This is the picture we need to have in our minds.

The final reason it's a bad idea to allow adversity to overshadow our prayers is simply that our spiritual life becomes dominated by the negative. Acts of Satan, instead of acts of God, fill up the horizon. We tend to become people who endure rather than overcome. With this mindset, times of prayer can get downright depressing. Granted, we're occupying enemy ground. Granted, terrible things do happen. But the best way to meet calamity is to focus on grace and praise and spiritual power and conversion—the positive, expansive acts of Christ in the world. Even in the midst of disaster, prayer can turn obstacles to our advantage. Let me illustrate.

Three interminable years of captivity had worn down the inmates of Kampili, a notorious women's prison camp the Japanese set up after their conquest of the Celebes Islands. World War II dragged on and on. Now a series of inexplicable bombing raids by the allies that hit the compound seemed the last straw. Many of the internees had become completely demoralized, most had grown apathetic; even the children became listless. Rainy days thumped out an endless monotony.

One prisoner, however, a former missionary to New Guinea named Darlene Deibler Rose, responded to the crisis by going on the offensive through prayer.[2] She petitioned the Lord on behalf of Mr. Yamaji, the brutal camp commander who could beat prisoners unmercifully when angered. One day, standing before him in his office, she had the opportunity to share a few words about the Almighty Creator who died for him. Tears ran down his cheeks and he rushed into an adjoining room. As Darlene prayed for his salvation, the commander wept uncontrollably. Thereafter Mr. Yamaji began to show kindness to her and even tried to improve camp conditions for everyone.

Darlene could easily have fixed on the unending disaster of imprisonment in her prayers: "Please get us out of here; end this horrible war!" She could have pounded on the door of mercy over and over, locked on the final solution. That would have been understandable under the circumstances. But God would have seemed quite distant during those years in Kampili, coming to the rescue someday, but not yet, not today, not tomorrow, not next week. . . . She would have found herself in that familiar plight: always crying out, never getting an answer. Instead Darlene concentrated on what God could do right there in camp. What stands out in this woman's recollections of that time were acts of providence that lit up the long night like a flare gun.

One day Darlene was called into the hospital where Rachel, a Jewish internee, lay gasping for breath, trying to fight off a serious asthma attack. She knelt by the bed and whispered, "Rachel, we pray to the same God. I'm going to pray for you now." The woman nodded. Darlene asked God to touch her body. "Immediately her breathing eased, and the following morning she returned to the barracks."

When the dreaded Kempeitai secret police took her to their prison, Darlene remembered the weapon of prayer. Her main request was that she would stand for Christ. As she prayed, "Strength came. . . . God gave me the courage to deport myself like a good soldier for my Lord before those cruel men."

Because Darlene petitioned aggressively, and not just defensively, she saw God's reassuring gestures even in the midst of disaster. One night she watched from her cell window as someone sneaked a bunch of bananas through a vine-covered fence to one of the native prisoners. Darlene dropped to the floor trembling, overcome by a craving: "Lord, just *one* banana." A little later she gave thanks contritely for her rice porridge.

The next morning a guard dropped a large cluster of bananas at her feet. Darlene slowly counted ninety-two of the precious fruit and heard God's note attached to the gift: "That's what I delight to do: the exceeding abundant above anything you ask or think."

Back at the compound, huddling with the other prisoners in huts because many barracks had been destroyed during weeks of air raids, Darlene prayed, "Please, Lord, for the sake of the children, let there be no air raid tonight. There's no moon and we don't know this area, so where would we hide?" The planes didn't come.

The Almighty was real and present for Darlene Deibler Rose in a place where He could have seemed agonizingly distant. She found Him in the here and now because she looked. Although Darlene longed for the end of the war as fervently as anyone, she refused to confine her hopes and prayers to that day of final deliverance. Her prison life was not dominated by disaster but propelled forward by two things: a continual endeavor to remain close to God and a continual awareness of His small favors. This was a woman who could look up at the stars from a bomb-blackened shelter and rejoice that the Creator of the heavens had entered into a relationship with her: "Oh, the wonder of His love for me and His personal concern for me, as an individual, was overwhelming."

In our first three chapters we've looked at a few practical tools that can reshape your prayers into something more answerable. You can begin using these tools immediately:

- Break down your big problems into smaller steps; become solution-centered in prayer.
- Move out of the Couch Potato School of Prayer and into setting up a rendezvous with God.

- Use prayer to learn from your trials—not just escape them.

Please start experimenting with these approaches. You'll soon find yourself becoming more enthusiastic and adventuresome about what may have previously been routine petition. There's nothing like feedback from God to get the juices flowing.

Now we're ready to move on to the three classic components of successful petition, three *how-to's* involving faith, persistence, and godliness that the New Testament emphasizes. Many believers have been intimidated by these "conditions" to answered prayer. But, as we'll see, the Bible shows clearly and simply how all of us can get there from here.

A failure of faith is
a failure of perspective.

CHAPTER FOUR

Faith Enough

"According to your faith will it be done to you."
"Woman, you have great faith! Your request is granted."
"Go your way, your faith has made you well."
"Your faith has saved you; go in peace."
"Don't be afraid; just believe, and she will be healed."[1]

Glancing through the gospel narratives in which Jesus responded to various requests for help, you soon catch a common theme. The Savior spotlighted faith as the key to a petitioner's answer. Many of the miracle stories climax in a statement about belief.

Once, while Jesus' disciples were staring wide-eyed at a fig tree that had withered at His command, the Master calmly assured them: "If you believe, you will receive whatever you ask for in prayer" (Matthew 21:22). This promise is so outrageous that we are inclined, at first sight, to check for loopholes; surely Jesus didn't really mean that.

When we claim great promises and find that our petitions are apparently unanswered, we naturally tend to fault our part of the agreement: faith. Jesus said, "If you believe, you will receive." Well, if we didn't receive we must not have believed enough. We'll try to have more faith next time.

This approach leaves a long list of casualties. Earnest Christians have made themselves sick trying to believe intensely enough. You try hard to have faith, don't get the answer desired, feel guilty; you try even harder, fail, feel even more guilty. It's possible, in fact, to drive yourself crazy trying to manufacture enough faith. How do you do it? Grunt? Squint? Repeat key phrases over and over?

Others opt simply to bow out. We hear statements like, "I wish I had faith like hers and could really pray"—the assumption being that some supernatural gift is required or an inherent gullibility that acknowledges the impossible as true. This kind of faith can appear to be removed some distance from anything the averge Christian experiences. So, many conclude it's only for the select few.

HEALTHY FAITH

To find a healthy response to Christ's emphasis on belief as the key to answered prayer, let's compare incidents in which He commended "great faith" with those in which He lamented "little faith."

A Roman centurion once approached Jesus in Capernaum and asked that his servant be healed. Jesus offered to go to the man's house. The centurion replied that this wasn't necessary; if the Master would just be good enough to utter a word, that was sufficient.

How could this soldier say such a thing? Because as a centurion he understood power and command. He knew he had the authority to order the troops under him to do his bidding. So he applied those facts to Christ. Abundant evidence confirmed that Jesus could perform miracles; wide testimony affirmed His authority to heal.

The centurion did not need an obvious display with dramatic gestures and incantations to prove Jesus' power. He simply drew a conclusion—a word of command from Jesus could result in healing—based on what he knew; he stretched his understanding to encompass the new idea of this great miracle worker. But the man wasn't stretching against the facts. He counted something as true because of the facts on hand. So Jesus, looking around at bystanders who often ignored or rejected evidence of His messiahship, declared, "I have not found anyone in Israel with such great faith" (Matthew 8:10).

The great faith commended by Christ simply reaches out on the basis of certain information and counts something about the Savior as true. In this case, the centurion acknowledged Jesus as the Healer and was rewarded.

Now to a vignette of faith on the rocks.

The disciples were crossing the Sea of Galilee when a furious squall came up and nearly swamped their boat. Looking around in desperation, they saw Jesus sleeping on a cushion in the stern. At this point the Twelve could have counted as true one of two things: (1) Jesus is calmly dozing because He is in control of the situation; (2) Jesus is calmly dozing because He doesn't care if we all drown.

These men had just witnessed demonstrations of Jesus' control over everything from the fish in the sea to deadly diseases like paralysis and leprosy. But in the panic of the moment they opted to count the second option as true. They shouted to their Master through the howling wind, "Teacher, don't you care if we drown?" (Mark 4:38).

Jesus roused Himself and told the cataclysmic elements to quiet down, which they did with remarkable promptness. Then He cast an eye around at His shivering disciples and asked, "Why are you so afraid? Do you still have no faith?" (verse 39).

To Jesus the lack of faith was always a surprise. We tend to be mystified by great faith. But for Him, belief was the natural response to His very clear and powerfully supported revelations. Why couldn't people draw the obvious conclusions?

The Twelve had not drawn the logical conclusion based on the facts they knew about Jesus. Instead they reacted with understandable but irrational fear. (Did they really

think this Man didn't care if they all went to the bottom?)
Christ defined this reaction as the opposite of faith.

On another occasion Jesus was sailing on the lake,
away from the carping Pharisees and toward the coast of
Bethsaida-Julius, when He dropped a rather abrupt warning on His disciples: "Be on your guard against the yeast of
the Pharisees and Sadduccees" (Matthew 16:6). The Twelve
began speculating about what this statement meant. Then
they hit on an answer: "Oh, we forgot to take a supply of
bread for the trip."

Dismay crept over Jesus' face, and He expressed His
disappointment with the words, "You of little faith." He had
just fed five thousand men and their families with five loaves,
and shortly before that four thousand ate their fill with seven
loaves Jesus blessed. Certainly an adequate supply of bread
was not the Master's primary concern. But the meaning of
these "signs" apparently did not sink in for the disciples.
Their minds were stuck on flour and dough and yeast and
had not yet become buoyant enough to focus on the spiritual
counterparts.

The lack of healthy faith that Jesus pointed out was
a failure of perspective, not a failure to believe something
difficult. Christ had just blown doubt out of the water by
multiplying bread for a multitude. The disciples fell short
of seeing spiritual meaning; their thoughts loitered on the
ground floor of reality.

The faith that Jesus so earnestly hopes to nurture
involves a point of view, a choice of what to focus on, picking
up on what really matters. Faith counts as true whatever
facts we have access to. If you have access to only a few facts,
that's okay, draw conclusions based on them.

The factor that makes the difference is this: exercising
whatever faith you have, instead of not exercising the faith
you don't have. It's the old glass of water question—is it half
empty or half full? You can either look at what God *hasn't*
done for you, or place your trust in what God *has* done for
you and go from there.

Jesus' assurance is that even with a mustard seed of faith we can begin a long and wonderful journey.

▼

WHY FAITH?

A visitor to Niels Bohr's country cottage was surprised to spot a horseshoe hanging on the wall. Wondering what use the brilliant physicist of quantum theory fame could possibly have for such an archaic superstition, he asked, "Can it be that you, of all people, believe it will bring you luck?"

"Of course not," Bohr replied, "but I understand it brings you luck whether you believe or not."

Recently, as I thought about this scientists's tongue-in-cheek remark, I began to question why prayer shouldn't be like his horseshoe. Why shouldn't God answer whether we believe or not? I began to wonder why Jesus emphasized faith so much.

An answer came when I realized what it would be like to petition the Lord without believing. What's the opposite of praying in faith? It's possible to toss a request up to God without counting anything as true. You pray just in case; it's like knocking on wood, can't hurt. When we pray like that, without any focus on God's ability or His truthfulness, our petitions tend to become mechanical—we pull a certain spiritual lever to see if anything will happen.

This kind of praying is unhealthy in the long run because it does not involve us on a deep level; we're not investing ourselves in any way. Part of the value of belief is that it helps us pray *to* God. Having faith in someone is not that different from giving yourself to someone. To believe as we pray is to invest ourselves in the petition: "I count this fact about God as true. I affirm His faithfulness." We're not whistling in the dark, we're praying *toward* the light. We're not just knocking on wood, we're knocking on the door of our Father's house.

To believe sincerely is also to desire something earnestly. Sometimes we rattle off a petition out of habit or a sense of

Are you knocking on the door,
or just knocking on wood?

duty without really having our heart in the request. God wants us to pray with desire, to concentrate on the object of our petition. Non-faith is as unhealthy, in its own way, as frantic attempts to manufacture faith. Non-faith doesn't count the important facts as true; it doesn't have a healthy focus of attention.

The Apostle James echoes Christ's emphasis on faith as the key to answered prayer in his statement about "the prayer offered in faith" making the sick person well (5:15). James also instructs us to believe and not doubt when we ask for wisdom. The latter remark may seem intimidating. Can we ever get to the point of not having any doubt about the requests we make to God? Must we believe so much that all uncertainty is somehow excluded?

James' point of view becomes clearer as he elaborates: "He who doubts is like a wave of the sea, blown and tossed by the wind. That man should not think he will receive anything from the Lord; he is a double-minded man, unstable in all he does" (1:6-7). Here James is equating doubt with being double-minded and unstable as a wind-tossed wave. This strongly suggests someone whose commitment is wishy-washy. A person comes to God and asks for wisdom or whatever, then turns around and forgets all about it; his desires drift elsewhere. A double-minded person can ask for one thing while thinking of something else quite the opposite.

James' point is that God does not reward that kind of flippant request. He does not typically dispense gifts to those who barely glance His way before rushing off somewhere else. William Temple wrote, "If all our wants are supplied while we have no thought of God, this may confirm us in our detachment from Him."

Healthy faith, on the other hand, fixes its gaze on the Object of belief. Think of the faith required of us in prayer as simply looking in the right direction. If our gaze is constantly jumping from here to there, then our faith can be faulted. But if we're honestly looking, that's enough. Our need is to concentrate on the Object of faith, not on generating a greater quantity of faith.

A Christian woman in Victorian London once wrote of a trying time in which she had to face a life-threatening illness.[2] Only major surgery could save her, a type of surgery that as often as not ended disastrously. For some time the woman could not bring herself to consent to the operation. She confessed, "I am a decided coward as to any inflicted pain." But after weighing the situation and realizing it was indeed a matter of life and death, she prayed her way to acceptance: "Never before, I think, was I enabled to put the whole thing so completely into the hands of our loving Lord."

Keeping this steady gaze, the woman requested two things from God: that she might not undergo the operation unless it was to be successful, and that she might not dishonor her Lord by fear. Afterward she wrote, "And emphatically were both petitions answered. *I had no fear whatever.* I talked of it as coolly as of any ordinary occurrence, with the full consciousness that there was something close by very dark, at which if I looked, for five minutes, I should be in perfect terror (I use the term advisedly); but if tempted so to do, there seemed a gentle whisper, that I was not to look at that, but at my loving Savior." She was kept "calm and peaceful, up to the last moment; more even to my own astonishment . . . than to that of my friends, because I alone knew my own cowardice."

Faith, for this woman, meant focusing on her loving Lord—and not on the terrors of the operation. Fear can constrict us terribly. Faith looks at something better. That's why we're asked to believe.

Knocking on wood or whistling in the dark doesn't do much for your perspective. But focusing your attention on God makes a difference—especially in times of trouble. If the problem is mesmerizing you and God has become a blob in the distance toward which you call, "If You can do anything," then your point of view needs to change. If you usually toss out requests without too much thought, or if your petitions are basically just in case, then a steadier gaze is in order.

To correct that faulty attention span, you don't have to become more credulous, you don't have to make yourself gullible, just look at whatever positive facts you have on hand about God. If you have a mustard seed of faith enough to believe God exists, then draw conclusions. Faith doesn't mean trying to look harder. It means counting something as true; it means investing yourself in the petition.

▼

HE IS ABLE

As Jesus was walking along a Galilean road with His usual crowd of followers, two blind men joined the throng and began shouting, "Have mercy on us, Son of David!" The men were calling out to Him as Messiah. When the party paused at a house for refreshment, the two managed to wedge their way close to Jesus and repeat their petition.

He asked, "Do you believe that I am able to do this?"

"Yes, Lord," they replied.

So Jesus gave them their sight, uttering a characteristic phrase: "According to your faith will it be done to you" (Matthew 9:27-30).

This is one of the very few passages that reveals what the needy person is supposed to believe, as opposed to simply commending faith. Of course the essential meaning of faith is to look at God Himself, to fix our gaze on Him. But here we see what, about God in particular, we are supposed to count as true. The blind men affirmed that Jesus was able to meet their needs.

On another occasion, a leper approached Jesus and said, "If you are willing, you can make me clean." The Master rewarded his faith immediately, cleansing him of his disease (Mark 1:40-42). The man reckoned as true what Jesus was capable of doing.

These incidents suggest something specific about how to pray in faith. It's best to phrase our request in terms of a positive statement about God.

Promises open us up
to possibilities.

When you ask, express your confidence in His ability. This is different from begging, "Please, please, please," or from trying to generate a greater quantity of faith, "I believe, I believe, I believe." You concentrate on God's ability. Your attention is focused on how big God is, *not* on how big (or small) your faith is.

The value of this kind of focus came through to me during an interminable Illinois winter. One morning I had to hand in a paper at the university I attended in order to pass a literature course. I managed to coax my frail Volkswagen through several miles of icy country road before coming to a long incline just beyond a narrow iron-frame bridge. I couldn't get any momentum going. Several times I skidded about a third of the way up, my bare tires spinning for traction in vain. There was no way I could make it. I began repeating "Lord, only by Your power can I do it, only by Your power." It was somewhat like an incantation, I admit, but I wanted to exercise faith instead of my bad temper. Just then a man came running out of the only house in sight, which had appeared deserted, jumped behind the car and pushed me all the way up.

Giving thanks, I steered on cheerfully and carefully until I ran into another long hill. I couldn't even get close to the top. Again I repeated, "Lord, only You can do it," trying to counter desperation with a clear focus. Just then my brother Dan came over the hill in his newer car (a vehicle that possessed real tires) on his way home from school. Dan's VW could make it back to school easily, and my car could make it down the slopes back to the house. We exchanged cars, turned around, and both arrived at our destinations. As I handed in my paper I couldn't help smiling about God's rather clever solutions.

Do you want to make your prayers more answerable? Make God bigger than your problems. Don't go on and on moaning about how terrible your situation is and begging God for His help. Instead go on and on about how wonderful God is and express confidence in His ability to help you.

This is a healthy, logical perspective in prayer. When you ask believing, you will receive.

POSSIBILITIES

Christ made outrageous promises about faith—laying them out bare and unqualified—in order to open us up to more possibilities. Much more is possible through the prayer of faith than we usually think. He wants to push us to experiment further, to attempt greater things. Jesus wanted to stretch His disciples, those men who were so slow to grasp the potential of the Kingdom and the spiritual meaning of Christ's every action. He was saying, in effect, "See more possibilities, draw more conclusions."

One practical way I have found to respond to Christ's outrageous promises and look intently in faith is simply to be more descriptive in prayer. That is, instead of just making a request, I describe exactly what I want God to do and affirm His specific intervention in some detail.

Sometimes desperation suggests such an approach. For instance, my six-month-old baby was crying almost all night for the second night in a row, and my wife was at the end of her rope and had fled with blankets to the living room. I groggily paced the bedroom, rocking Jason in my arms and keeping up a soothing monologue. He finally stopped screaming and closed his eyes. I laid him down in nerve-racking slow motion. Would he wake up again? Bending over the crib, I prayed that God would give him a restful night . . . and went on, claiming God's peace over him, the peace that passes all understanding and keeps our hearts and minds. Calling on this quality, sculpting it with words from Scripture over his tiny form under the blue comforter, I continued affirming the Holy Spirit's activity, and also (again moved by desperation) submitted myself to serve all night if necessary, to be patient.

Jason didn't wake up the rest of the night, which was quite unusual considering the circumstances. The next night we got off to an unpromising start, with our baby exercising his lungs several times before midnight. But at that dark hour I approached God with the same kind of descriptive, expressive prayer, and Jason didn't wake again until 5:30 a.m.

Eloquence in prayer, of course, doesn't guarantee the answer we desire. But I do believe God responds more effectively when we reach out wholeheartedly, fixing our gaze. In my experiences with descriptive prayer, I wasn't straining to manufacture more faith; I was celebrating the Object of faith. Positive, expressive prayer is the healthy alternative to flat-footed requests in which belief becomes indistinguishable from wishful thinking.

To exercise our faith and our imagination in prayer is to stand on tiptoe before the enormous sky of God's generosity. And our Lord, in turn, delights to stretch out of the blue and into our lives.

Agnes, where are my keys!!?

Turn shouts into whispers.

CHAPTER FIVE

Praying Through

DWIGHT L. MOODY used to tell a story about a Christian wife who persevered in prayer for her persistently unbelieving husband. At one point she resolved to pray for him every day at noon for eighteen months. That time passed and her knock at Heaven's gate had failed to prompt any observable response. So she exclaimed, "Lord, I will pray for him every day, and at all hours, as long as life lasts." That same day the husband was converted. Moody drew a lesson: "When the Lord saw that her faith would not give up, he sent the answer immediately."

The notion that we prevail upon the Lord by hanging tough with our petition is not a very attractive one at first sight. It seems manipulative. But perseverance in prayer is an unavoidable New Testament theme.

Christ once told His disciples a rather unpleasant story about a widow who kept pestering an indifferent judge, demanding justice against the person who had wronged her. The judge finally acceded to her request just to get the woman off his back. The point of the parable is that we "should always pray and not give up" (Luke 18:1-8). If an indifferent human judge can be persuaded to do the right thing by persistent petition, then surely our heavenly Sovereign, who has a passion for justice, can be moved by our pleas. So keep praying.

This parable is echoed in another, also recorded by Luke, about a man who comes at midnight to bang on the door of his friend's house, asking for bread to feed an unexpected guest. The last thing the one rudely awakened wants to do is get out of bed. But his "friend" keeps calling out until his request is granted. After telling the story, Jesus uttered His famous promise about asking, seeking, and knocking (11:5-10). The clear inference is that we should continue doing so until we get an answer.

Then there's the other side of the coin.

Jesus, who introduced this idea of persistence in prayer, also gives us a word of caution. During His Sermon on the Mount, He told the assembled multitude that secret prayer to God alone, as opposed to public prayer for show, is what really matters. And He added, "When you pray, do not keep on babbling like pagans, for they think they will be heard because of their many words. Do not be like them, for your Father knows what you need before you ask him" (Matthew 6:7-8).

Jesus warned His followers against a quantitative approach to prayer: the idea that repeating our petitions will inevitably bring an answer from God. Well, then, we might ask, what about the widow pestering the judge and the obnoxious man bugging his friend until he got out of bed? Those parables are supposed to teach us about prayer. Don't they suggest a babbling that expects to be heard because of many words?

It will help us understand if we see that those parables *and* Jesus' word of caution end on the same note. After talking about the widow, Jesus says that God the Judge is far more eager to dispense justice than any human official. After talking about the midnight caller, Jesus says that our heavenly Father is even more eager to give good gifts to us than a human father is to his child. And then, after warning about babbling, Jesus says our Father knows our need before we ask.

Seemingly opposite expositions arrive in the end at the same point. We are urged to persist in petition because God is so eager to give. We are warned against persistent babbling because God already knows (and by implication is eager to give).

Obviously there's a healthy kind of persistence and an unhealthy kind. The key difference relates to that common conclusion: God's generosity. Why we persist in prayer makes a big difference. The pagans Jesus mentioned as bad examples of prayer went on and on petitioning because they thought their god had to be talked into doing good; they assumed that a certain quantity of prayer would create some kind of cosmic coercion, forcing their god's hand. In the back of their minds, they believed he was lazy or indifferent and had to be prodded into action.

A young man named Steve Kemperman gives a contemporary glimpse into this kind of prayer. He wrote about a spiritually frustrating time with the Unification Movement in this way: "For two years I battled the denizens of the evil spiritual cloud bank, babbling and roaring my prayers . . . into the lonely nights of campground forests and secluded city lots." The reason for that kind of persistence was a certain Moonie supposition: "By praying fervently, even pounding, shouting and screaming prayers, you can eventually pay enough indemnity to break through the evil spiritual world to God. When you begin crying and feeling 'God's aching and grieving heart,' you've broken through."

One evening while "holed up in the Cleveland Center's whitewashed prayer room," Steve began looking through a book that expounded on the New Testament story of the prodigal son. As he visualized this father sitting on the porch, waiting eagerly for the delinquent son's return, and then running to embrace him, Steve broke through to something quite different: "Jesus' parable showed me in a few minutes what two-and-a-half years of search and struggle . . . had *not* shown me—the all-embracing . . . unconditional nature of God's love." This young man felt comforted by a God who now seemed very close. "From that day on I stopped screaming my prayers like a hyena with stomach cramps and began talking softly with the God who lived inside. There was no need to shout. He wasn't lingering on the other side of an evil spiritual world *waiting* for my arrival. Rather, each time I came to Him in prayer, I knew He'd come rushing to meet me, and to embrace me in the warmth of His arms."[1]

Unhealthy persistence attempts to earn favor with God by its loud and painful exertions. Healthy persistence begins with God's favor. As Christians we are to persist in prayer precisely because we understand God's eagerness to give good gifts. But this raises a question: If our Father doesn't need to be talked into anything, why persist in asking?

Remember that healthy faith in prayer is essentially a matter of looking at God's ability or His solutions. We can't look harder, but we can look steadily, avoiding distractions. I believe persistence is simply an extension of this kind of looking. God wants us to persist because He wants us to keep gazing in the right direction. Keeping our focus of attention on the good facts of faith is healthy.

Another reason for persistence is the fact that we're all involved in a struggle with forces of darkness. Even quixotic Moonie theology contains a grain of truth. The earth is not a neutral playing field. We're trapped on a planet that is in rebellion against God. As participants in the conflict between Christ and Satan, we have a role to play in extending God's hand in the world. We can create more room in which He may work.

During the terrifying first days of the Civil War, Henry Ward Beecher urged congregations to pray for their divided and bloodied country. He reported that, in the town of Norwood, every household was swept up in a reviving intercession: "By faith they laid their hearts upon the bosom of God, till they felt the beatings of that great Heart whose courses give life and law to the Universe."

Our persistence, our steady gaze, magnifies the possibilities for divine intervention. But again, we persist not because God is reluctant, but because He is zealous to act on our behalf. The Sovereign Lord longs to intervene in human life, but He has committed Himself to do so primarily by invitation. Our persistence bonds with divine eagerness to sabotage the dominion of evil on this planet.

▼

HOW WE PERSIST

French statesman Georges Clemenceau loathed traveling by plane and tried to avoid it whenever possible. Before one unavoidable flight he was heard to admonish the pilot sternly, "Fly very cautiously, very slow, and very low."

If you've found that your persistent petitions fall to the ground like stalled airplanes, take a closer look at how you're flying them. Some things build up momentum.

Joy and Thankfulness

When you look closely at the New Testament texts that deal with persistent prayer, you discover its most common companions: joy and thankfulness. The Apostle Paul's abundance of prayer, for example, flowed in a current of rejoicing:

> I have not stopped giving thanks for you, remembering you in my prayers.
> In all my prayers for all of you, I always pray with joy.
> We always thank God . . . when we pray for you.[2]

The flood of prayer that brims over in the epistles is full-spirited, a joyful fountain ascending. But here's the catch: Believers can pray joyfully only when we aim at a positive goal. Only that is sustainable. We tend to burn out when our petitions are aimed at the negative thing we're trying to avoid. Constantly asking God, "Get me out of this situation; remove this problem from my life," tends to turn prayer into

To hit more of the target, aim more at the center of God's will.

a chronic whine. There are certainly times when all we can do is yell for help, as the psalmist did when "down in the pit," but that should not be our long-term prayer mindset. We end up staring at the wrong things.

Dr. William Parker (whose fascinating prayer experiment is examined in chapter 7) wrote this summary of a group of volunteers who consistently failed in their petitions: "We found [them] using negative prayer, that is holding their unhappy symptoms directly in the focus of their attention. Over and over they declare they are unhappy, suffering, sinful and unworthy. Though these affirmations of misery were addressed to Our Father, still nothing, absolutely nothing happened to contradict them. They went right on being unhappy, ill, sinful just as they held they were." Parker concluded, "Negative prayer will produce negative results. It is ridiculous to blame either God or prayer power."[3]

Sometimes finding a positive goal is just a matter of rephrasing our prayer. Instead of pleading, "Save me from the horrible depression that's besieging me," we can ask, "Show me something to be thankful for today, Lord. Help me to see You in my world." Instead of whining about doubt, pray about your faithful Savior Jesus. Instead of pleading that a troublesome coworker be removed, pray for patience and understanding. Instead of just agonizing about lust, aim at purity and sensitivity.

How long should you persist? As long as you can do so joyfully. If your persistence has become a gripe session, a way to vent frustration, or a grim struggle after an elusive goal, then stop—something's wrong. Don't let perseverance degenerate into a tug-of-will between you and a seemingly indisposed Father in Heaven. If you are moved to persist in prayer, find something positive to persist about. Express hope, not just desperation.

Center of God's Will

God's promises in the Bible are another means of checking our persistence to see if it's on the right track. What our

Lord promises most is a good indication of His priorities, and answerable prayer tends to follow those priorities. It's best to aim long and hard at what God has promised longest and hardest. If your persistent petitions usually run into a dead end, ask yourself if what you aim at most earnestly is on the periphery of God's will.

For example, our Father is effusive when it comes to commands and assurances about loving our neighbor. We can know that requests to better love someone are aimed at the center of His will. Likewise, promises about God removing our fears, filling us with the Spirit, giving us power to witness, and enlightening our minds are explicit and numerous. Since these things also lie in the center of God's will we can pursue them with confident persistence.

Other targets are much more dependent on circumstances. God has promised to bless us abundantly, but a new Buick may or may not be included in that package deal. We can find promises related to healing, but a cure for our present physical affliction may or may not be best in the long run.

Not all blessings are created equal. Some lie at the very heart of God's plan for us; others function like the limbs of a body, which can be used for good or ill. Of course, it's not wrong to pray for a new car or an end to a headache or a promotion or a host of other specific benefits. On occasion we may find reason to, or be impressed to, pursue these targets energetically in prayer. But as a rule, it's not a good idea to persist most after what God has promised least.

Persistent prayer should be a way of stretching our desires toward the God we love, not an exercise in constricting our desires around the object almost in hand. The thing to get should never be the one unchanging element in the prayer equation. Our desire to interact with God must be the one constant. So remember to keep looking in prayer, keeping the focus of faith on the Giver, not just on what He may give.

A distressed mother once came to see H. Clay Trumbull with a sad story.[4] Her son had wandered from the faith into a dissipated life. She'd prayed earnestly and constantly for him and after a time he had come back into the church and even become an active Christian worker. This, of course, had made her ecstatic. But now her son had fallen back into his old habits and apparently lost his faith. He'd left home, enlisted in the navy, and sailed to the Orient.

The woman had just about lost her confidence in the value of persistent prayer. She didn't think she could have as much ground for hope in prayer now as she had when her son was an active believer.

"Is the difference in God or in your boy?" Trumbull asked her.

"It's in my boy. That's what's troubling me."

"On whom did your faith rest when your boy was doing his best?"

"On God of course."

"And has God changed?"

At length this despairing woman caught the point. "Do you mean to suggest that even now, while my poor boy is in his present state, I can look up to God, and pray for my boy as trustfully as I prayed while he was active in Christian work?"

Precisely, the pastor told her, emphasizing, "But you must look to God, and not at your boy, while you pray."

The mother decided to do just that, and found her way to a healthy kind of persistence. In this case, her renewed prayers coincided with her son's dramatic reconversion on board ship in Chinese waters.

▼

KNOCKING AND LISTENING

Admittedly, a tension exists between becoming malleable in prayer and at the same time fulfilling that call to persevere. When do we seek to know God's will, and when do we claim it? When do we submit ourselves (the prayer of relinquishment), and when do we confidently ask (the prayer of faith)?

When does persistence become presumption?

Here's Andrew Murray's response to that question. After asserting that it is the rule in the Father's family that "every childlike believing petition is granted" he wrote, "If no answer comes, we are not to sit down in the sloth that calls itself resignation, and suppose that it is not God's will to give an answer. No, there must be something in the prayer that is not as God would have it, childlike and believing; we must seek for grace to pray so that the answer may come."

Andrew Murray qualified this answer by stating that God will tell us when a request is not according to His will "as when Moses asked to enter Canaan." Then we are to submit "even as the Son did in Gethsemane." He advised, "Let us withdraw the request, if it be not according to God's mind, or persevere till the answer come."[5]

In the end, answerable persistence is a matter of the heart and its openness to God. If we make an honest and regular attempt to listen to Him, then our chances of being on the right track improve tremendously. Investing time in devotional prayer and Bible study each day creates the environment in which spiritual learning occurs. We need to make sure that our petitions, especially the persistent ones, are part of this communion with God and not something isolated from it. In other words, be sure you're talking (and listening) while you're knocking. Don't wait for the answer in silence.

A text in Hebrews hints at this process at work in Christ's life: "During the days of Jesus' life on earth, he offered up prayers and petitions with loud cries and tears to the one who could save him from death, and he was heard because of his reverent submission" (5:7). This last phrase seems a contradiction. If He was reverently submitting, what was there to hear? Surely no loud petitions.

Evidently petition and submission go together. Those loud cries and tears grew out of a teachable attitude. To use a metaphor: Submitting to God's will is the soil from which the plants of petition spring up. First, we cultivate a responsiveness to the Father; we loosen up our desires and goals.

Then, guided by biblical promises and experiential feedback, we plant the seeds of faith—specific requests—and nurture them by persistence.

Neither half of this process works without the other. If we spend all our time hoeing the ground—seeking God's will, but never asking for anything—then our submission shrivels into a passive abstraction. Nothing grows as a result. And if we try to plant in unprepared soil—asking, asking, asking—our requests have little chance of bearing any fruit.

No exhaustive formulas exist for persisting correctly, just as no hard and fast rules apply to every situation in life. We need God's very present help in all our decisions.

NIGHT WATCH

I'll never forget the day I walked into a hospital room where my father lay after he'd suffered a severe stroke. I stared in shock as Barbara, Dad's bride of a few weeks, hovered over him, trying desperately to keep his air passage clear. It was his terrible fight for breath, chest and abdomen heaving with hardly a second's rest, that most unnerved me. But I managed to jump into the fray, white-faced and trembling, and try to get the tube down deeper to the deadly, ever-forming mucus. I watched his eyes roll and his head shake in vain. His limbs were weak, his moans strong.

During a pause in Dad's struggle, two of his friends dropped by. This Pentecostal couple told us they'd been praying for his complete recovery and were certain of a prompt answer. As these two earnest souls leaned over and greeted Dad, they saw, or imagined, a positive response to their presence and prayers in his loud, uneven breath. Standing by the bedside they touched him tenderly and seized hope in the occasional twitch of his limbs. They whispered excitedly that Dad raised his hand while they were petitioning the Lord.

After they left, Barbara told me the doctor had given instructions to the floor nurses not to resuscitate Dad should he stop breathing. I wanted to know why.

When the physician came in I asked, "So what are his chances of recovering?"

"I would say almost none."

"You're saying his brain is dead?"

"Well, even if he recovers from the pneumonia . . . you must think of what you are going to have left. In order to recover, your father must regain basic functions. He must be able to swallow, to eat; he must be truly alert, recognize people. Otherwise he will be just a vegetable, I'm afraid."

I wanted to know exactly what the brain scan revealed.

"Well, a brain scan doesn't really tell you about the future," the doctor answered. "Some people with minor damage never recover. Others with half their brain gone still function normally. The key is function—the ability to eat and be alert."

When Barbara mentioned the pastor planned to come at 3:00 for an anointing service, I wondered how I should pray. To me, an "if it be Thy will" petition was very near to no petition at all. I was quite willing to wield hard-hitting promises and pound on the door of the Lord like the persistent widow in Jesus' parable. But I didn't want Dad to suffer pointlessly. I was also willing to cooperate and give him into God's hands. Should I fight in petition, or should I rest in submission?

For some reason, looking at Dad's heaving thorax, I didn't want to settle for a safe medium. I wanted to go one way or the other. After praying about how to pray, I recalled the doctor's words concerning function. Maybe that could be a sign. We could ask God to give us an indication about how He wanted us to pray. It wouldn't be something arbitrary.

There were two specific things: swallowing and recognizing people. If we saw a bit of progress in these areas then we would know to petition for recovery all the way in earnest. If not, we would prayerfully rest in God's will. Barbara and I had a long talk about this and agreed that our part in the anointing would be to ask for these particular signs.

Our minister and an elder arrived—old friends of the family. The pastor took his tiny bottle of oil and rubbed a little on Dad's furrowed forehead. He placed a hand on his numb shoulder and began to pray quietly, just laying things out for God's will. I couldn't help thinking how this good man's conservative faith contrasted with that of the Pentecostal couple. I wondered which faith I would have to exercise in the end—even as I pleaded for that sign of hope.

My brothers arrived late in the afternoon and said they would stay with Dad while I went out for a bite to eat. I persuaded Barbara to take a break too. When we returned to the hospital, Jerry and Dan reported that Dad had slept awhile, breathing rather restfully for the first time. It was exhilarating news.

That night my brothers and I kept a vigil in room 309, watching over the helpless man who once changed our diapers. He still heaved sometimes, but was definitely sleeping more than struggling. On occasion he snoozed quietly. His shallow, but regular breathing sounded wonderful.

About 10:00 Sunday morning, after a few hours of sleep, Dan, Jerry, and I returned to the hospital. Nurses had disconnected the oxygen. Dad was breathing just fine on his own. They believed he'd licked the pneumonia. One said, "A miracle is just what we needed around here."

I walked over to the bed; Dad saw me and smiled. I grabbed on to the faint twinkle in his eyes for all I was worth. A good sign. Then he asked for water. I held a paper cup to his lips, he gulped, and swallowed—yes, swallowed twice. We were jubilant. Two good signs. I remembered that I could pound on the door now without reservation. But of course I'd jumped the gun and already begun petitioning very eagerly.

We spent the day congratulating Dad on his imminent recovery and exercising the languid limbs on his paralyzed right side. Each of us spotted more signs of recognition in his eyes. That night my brothers and I took turns keeping watch at the hospital. Dad slept like a baby.

Pray with both hands.

CHAPTER SIX

Godly Momentum

WHILE WORKING AT the Christian English school in Japan, I proposed in a staff meeting that we ask God to pack the church at our next series of evangelistic meetings. I was tired of seeing the evangelist preach to a smattering of guests in a sea of empty chairs. The vacant seats spoke more loudly than the minister. It was absurd.

Wasn't Almighty God searching through the metropolis of Osaka for potential children? Surely out of six million souls He could gather a few hundred seekers and bring them around to our meetings. The time seemed right. We student missionaries had grown close as a group. Having to make God real to people for whom He was a complete stranger had challenged and revitalized our faith. We had been claiming Bible promises to good effect. A godly momentum was building up our expectations.

So we began praying, claiming promises, asking specifically that God show His hand and fill all the seats. This was His work; winning people was His will; we were united in His name.

We sent out invitations, put up signs—and kept praying.

Opening night we swung back the doors, believing. The evangelist spoke . . . and his voice echoed back from hundreds of empty chairs.

It was a long train ride home that night. At 10:00 p.m. the drunks were trying to make it back to studio apartments. The workaholics stared across the aisle more blankly than ever. Amid the monotonous clack of the rails, I felt terribly alone. I had to change trains at Nishinomiya station. While waiting for my train, I walked out to the end of the platform. The city lights spread to the horizon. I looked up and pondered the dark, blank sky.

God hadn't answered our modest call. Where was the Almighty? Our efforts to speak for Him in that place seemed painfully feeble. We hadn't even made a ripple. The millions just walked on by.

PETITION SHORT-CIRCUITED

Those empty chairs at our evangelistic series bothered me for some time. I found it quite unusual for such a highly motivated request to go so completely unanswered. Some years after I returned to the United States from my assignment, I made a surprising discovery. I learned that two of the unmarried teachers had had a sexual relationship at the time we were petitioning the Lord for a packed house.

I recalled that those two had been less than enthusiastic about boldly claiming Bible promises for a person in every seat. Now I realized why. There was a barrier in their minds, an uneasiness about marching right up to the throne of grace.

Apparently, our petition as a group just couldn't go through. In that instance, sin short-circuited God's power. We were not fully grounded in grace. Sin (the transgression of God's Law) somehow prevented Him from doing what He is, according to the Bible, very eager to do.

Human sin is undeniably a part of the problem of unanswered prayer. The Old Testament emphasizes this factor the most. Speaking to people who were openly corrupt and deliberately apostate, the prophet Isaiah explained:

> "But your iniquities have separated
>   you from your God;
> your sins have hidden his face from you,
>   so that he will not hear." (59:2)

On another occasion Isaiah quoted the Almighty's response to a people who combined pious observances with greed and oppression:

> "When you spread out your hands in prayer,
>   I will hide my eyes from you;
> even if you offer many prayers,
>   I will not listen." (1:15)

Sin makes God flee from our prayers as from a disconcerting noise. But the plain fact is, we all engage in sinful behavior. If prayers were answered only for the sinless, the Father would have hung up the phone after Jesus said His last Amen on earth. However, according to wide testimony, He is still very much on the line.

Looking back on that experience in Japan, I realize that the rest of us in that group did not expect an answer because of any special merit we possessed. Each of us had our imperfections and our obvious faults. But two people were involved in deliberate disobedience. Regularly and with premeditation, they carried out something they knew was wrong. I think that put up a barrier.

It wasn't that God found their particular sin especially odious and so turned away in disgust. The problem was, the Almighty could not bless willful defiance.

Deliberate sin separates people from God. There's no getting around it. Sin is a humanly insurmountable barrier, breached only by the heroic sacrifice of Christ. That might be hard for us to grasp in a world permeated by evil. Sin does not come to us as some hideous stranger. It's a warm, familiar friend. We tend to cozy up to it just as fast as we can.

But for God it is an outrage that cuts Him off from us. He cannot act, or more accurately, He cannot act and still be just. Our access to His power is short-circuited by sin. It can actually make Him appear unresponsive and our prayers seem like a whistling in the dark.

In His Sermon on the Mount, Jesus advised, "Therefore, if you are offering your gift at the altar and there remember that your brother has something against you, leave your gift there in front of the altar. First go and be reconciled to your brother; then come and offer your gift" (Matthew 5:23). Here the suggestion is of something specific that needs to be made right. Rather than submerge the problem under religious activity, we must attempt to solve it.

The Apostle James echoed this idea: "Therefore confess your sins to each other and pray for each other so that you may be healed" (5:16). Clearing up the lines of communication down here opens up the lines extending heavenward.

Unconfessed sin ticking away in our souls, which we attempt to drown out by turning up the volume on other things, will detonate at some point. We can't play games with the One who sees into our innermost selves. Making our prayers more answerable involves making ourselves more transparent before our heavenly Father.

▼

LEVEL OF PERFORMANCE

Rosalind Goforth's four-year-old daughter, Gracie, was dying in China of an enlarged spleen. Missionary doctors could do nothing. Neither could they help the sick child of a Christian Chinese woman who came to the clinic and beseeched them pitifully. The Chinese mother desperately pleaded, declaring her unlimited faith in the Western physicians, until Mr. Goforth finally pointed to little Gracie, who was about the

We all come boldly
for the same reason.

same age as the woman's son, and told her, "Surely, if the doctor cannot save our child, neither can he save yours; your only hope and ours is in the Lord Himself."

The woman took this not as a word of doom but as a ray of hope. She committed her child into the Lord's hands and felt assured he would recover. Two weeks later she called on Mrs. Goforth with exhilarating news: Her little boy was well; the doctor could discover nothing wrong with him.

The Goforths, of course, were also praying, as only parents can who must watch their child suffer. But Gracie died. Mrs. Goforth was left with an agonizing question: Why wasn't her child spared? For some time this devout and deeply grieved mother could find no answer. But later, in writing about the experience, she would grope for one: "I do know that there was in my life, at that time, the sin of bitterness toward another, and an unwillingness to forgive a wrong. This was quite sufficient to hinder any prayer, and did hinder for years, until it was set right."[1]

Mrs. Goforth's admission is so heart-rending it compels us to look for some other explanation. Was this a genuinely cherished resentment, or was she simply casting about for some moral flaw that might have impeded her petition? It's hard to believe that as this godly missionary earnestly petitioned her Lord, she didn't notice this hard spot of animosity in her heart. Surely she would have dealt with any discernible problem right then—no matter the cost.

In any case, the idea of God allowing a child to die because of a fault in the mother makes us cringe. Think of what an incredible load of guilt this could create: My unforgiving spirit killed my child. A less-balanced person might have been destroyed by it. Fortunately, Mrs. Goforth was able in the end to accept the denial of her petition as what must be best in the long run. She fell back on her own experience as a parent: "We see it best to grant at one time what we withhold at another."

Our Father wants us to deal with sin. But we have to be careful that our openness toward Him doesn't turn into endless, gloomy introspection. Some perfectionist people descend into faultfinding detours that compound their sense of guilt and inadequacy.

Bringing transgressions out on the table is the Holy Spirit's duty; we don't have to crawl around under it. Our job is simply to be still and observe. We expose ourselves to the Word; we listen carefully; we become transparent in prayer. The mistakes fatal to petition involve *clinging* to sin, *avoiding* the pointed remarks of God's Word and Spirit. The Apostle John offers us a good rule of thumb: "Dear friends, if our hearts do not condemn us, we have confidence before God and receive from him anything we ask, because we obey his commands and do what pleases him" (1 John 3:21-22).

It's unwise to tie answered prayer to a certain level of performance. Trying to be holier in order to get more from God is self-defeating; it turns us into pious manipulators. Some earnest believers react to unanswered prayer by saying, "I need to be more loving to my spouse," or "Oh, I really should witness more." The hope is that if they could just lose their temper less this week, or slip in a few more good words for the Lord, maybe He would answer. But this can never produce assurance. There is always something more we could be doing for God. We could pray more, study the Bible more, help the poor more. In short, we'll never measure up—all the way.

Never let the distance you haven't yet traveled toward God become a barrier; God certainly doesn't. He came all the way down to meet us at our lowest point via the cross. He understands what it's like to be tempted and bent out of shape. Most importantly, He has taken care of our falling short by His own righteous life poured out graciously to the unworthy from Calvary.

We come boldly before the throne of grace and gain access to God's attentive ear for one reason, and one reason alone: the merit of Jesus Christ. We enter into that inner sanctum in Someone else's name today and will enter exactly the same way no matter what we accomplish in the future. In Jesus' parable, the tax collector pleading his unworthiness, not the Pharisee presenting his accomplishments, got a favored hearing.

A FIGHTING LINE

Days after D-Day in Normandy, C. S. Lewis was thinking about the small bite taken out of Nazi-occupied Europe by the Allied armies and realized how this illustrated our individual progress in faith. He wrote, "There is, we have to admit, a line of demarcation between God's part in us and the enemy's region. But it is, we hope, a fighting line; not a frontier fixed by agreement."[2]

None of us obeys the commands of our Lord perfectly. We never reach a point where we no longer need the substitution of the One made righteousness for us. But we do need to follow Christ into the next battle. A sincere commitment to obey Him is what counts. That should clear away any obstacles to fluid prayer. We'll find that answers multiply when we're seeking to do the right thing.

A man with a reputation for a dissolute lifestyle came to Christ and, as often happens, received a "new and improved" conscience. A debt of $18.75, which before had not troubled him in the slightest, now loomed large. However, he was almost penniless, and eighteen dollars was a considerable sum at that time. This new Christian decided to phone his creditor. He urged him to come and pick up a bureau, table, and mirror to cover the debt. But the creditor declined and said he could wait until November 18 for payment.

The new believer was still unable to earn or find the money by the deadline. He spent the night of the seventeenth in earnest prayer that God would enable him to fulfill his responsibility. The man felt assured that "He knoweth how to deliver."

On his way to work in the morning, he was accosted by the proprietor of a large store. "For three days," he said, "I have been impressed with the idea that I must give you $18.75, and for three days have been trying to ascertain why I must give you this amount, for I do not owe any man a penny. I cannot get rid of the thought, and if you value my peace of mind, I beg you take the money!"[3]

▼

BUILDING MOMENTUM

Renowned evangelist Dwight Moody once took on the chairman of the Edinburgh Infidel Club in a public debate. The atheist mocked when the evangelist knelt down and prayed for him, but Moody told him cheerfully, "God's time will come. There are a great many praying for you." Six months later Moody got a letter stating that the "infidel" had come to Christ and brought seventeen of his former club members with him.[4]

John Wesley once took on the blazing sun. He was speaking in a field crowded with people eager to hear him present the gospel. The heat grew so intense that he could hardly continue preaching. Wesley lifted up his heart to God and, "in a minute or two [the sun] was covered with clouds, which continued till the service was over."[5]

Charles Finney took on a drought. Dark clouds dumped their rain over the lake near Oberlin College and left the farm land along the shore parched and barren. This happened for three months. A skeptical acquaintance asked Finney why this wise and good God he was always talking about would waste such a quantity of rain where it could do no good and allow the farmers to suffer terribly.

Cut to the heart, Finney rushed home to his closet, reminded God of all the prayers for rain, and suggested that, to bring honor to His name, the time for an answer was now. A strong wind began blowing before Finney had risen from his knees, the heavy clouds rolled over, and rain fell on land "two full hours."[6]

We've tried to avoid making any measure of performance

a condition for answered prayer. But it does seem that miracles do adhere to certain men and women of God—as if they were magnetized in some way. Some saints attract much more than their share of the prizes of providence. Do they have some secret? Does God play favorites?

In his epistle, James observed, "The prayer of a righteous man is powerful and effective" (5:16). How do we reconcile this with the idea that trying do more good (or less bad) in order to get more answers from God is a dead end? To understand James's point better, look at the example he gives: the prophet Elijah, a "man just like us," who single-handedly turned off and on the rain by earnest prayer. Elijah actually was praying for a sign that would convict his contemporaries of their need to return to the covenant with God.

This prophet wasn't making a request for personal need— a place to sleep that night or more amiable disciples—he was praying as a public intermediary between God and the people who had betrayed Him. As such, his position as a "righteous" man, a man sincerely following Yahweh, had great importance.

In thinking about the "effective" prayers of the "righteous," the first thing to note is the distinction between private petitions and prayers to accomplish God's work in the world. Think of the mother praying for her sick child or someone pleading for a job. With such requests, our need is our only argument, and God's protective love is the key to an answer. Prayers for personal needs relate to the model of a father and his child. It's hard to see the petitioner's spiritual power entering the picture.

But then think of asking that people will flock to an evangelistic meeting or that a ministry to the homeless will prosper. Here biblical examples suggest the model of master and servant. Some servants are more efficient and productive than others; some have ten talents, others five. In carrying out God's work in the world, a person's spiritual power is a relevant factor.

Servant-leaders who remain committed to their tasks

certainly play key roles in extending God's plan. Their righteous lives are an integral part of their effectiveness. All of us
who seek to carry out God's will play a similar role, though
not on the same scale. So our personal holiness has rele-
vance. Our spiritual potency increases in direct proportion to
our closeness to God. That affects everything: our influence,
our witness, our behavior, and our prayers.

If this sounds like a formidable calling, here's good news:
The spiritual power that enables prayer to have more of an
impact for God in the world isn't something that has to be
accumulated over the years like a savings account. It isn't
merit built up by a long string of good deeds. Spiritual power
is a matter of momentum. And momentum, as opposed to
level of achievement, can happen right now.

It's interesting to note, as you look at spiritual biogra-
phies, that a person's most memorable answers to prayer
often cluster around the time during and just after conversion. That's when our world pulsates with blessing. Why?
Because that's when we have spiritual momentum; we're
moved by God to a new point, propelled more directly by
grace, drawn more distinctly by divine love. And that appears
to be the optimum environment for answerable prayer.

At one point during my missionary tour in Japan, almost
all the teachers at the Osaka English Language School were
laboring with one student, Junko, who seemed just about to
make a commitment to Christ. But she kept stepping back,
just out of reach, because of that perennial problem: hypo-
crites in the church. We all prayed for Junko and several of
us talked with her. The collective message was: Stop looking
at people, and focus on Christ.

But we weren't getting through. As a two-year veteran,
I imagined that my theological insights would carry the day
when I sat down with Junko in the Bible classroom and
carefully explained why Christ alone must be the center of
our lives as Christians. She smiled politely—and stared back
blankly.

Then a teacher named Sonya had a talk with the girl.

This was the young woman I described in chapter 1, who had wilted into a chair beside me and confessed her utter failure as a missionary. But the most vulnerable person I'd ever known had begun to make exciting discoveries in the Word. God was speaking to her as her Present Companion. Her devotional life had come alive, and she was sharing quite effectively in Bible classes.

That's when frail little Sonya spoke with Junko. She told her to stop looking at people and focus on Christ— exactly what the rest of us had said. But this time Junko was struck by a revelation. She replied enthusiastically, "Yes, that's what I need to do!" The good word finally broke through.

Spiritual power is not based on seniority, promotion through the ranks, or a lengthy résumé. It's the state of the heart, right now. It's momentum. To pray earnestly with intensity is in itself a part of the righteousness that accomplishes much. A desire for God, a longing to please Him welling up in our hearts, can make things happen. This present-tense closeness is in Jesus' great promise about prayer: "If you remain in me and my words remain in you, ask whatever you wish, and it will be given you" (John 15:7-8). Abiding in Christ begins today, this morning. It's an instant connection. And spiritual power is the result.

God wants to make us spiritually successful *right now*. That's the key to the three classic components of healthy petition we've covered in the last three chapters. We don't have to sit around waiting and hoping that faith, persistence, and godliness will show up someday. They are resources we can plug into today. Start practicing:

- A healthy faith that counts facts on hand as true and makes God bigger than the problem.
- A joyful persistence focused on a positive goal in the center of God's will.
- A present seeking of God: honest about your failings, serious about His calling.

These elements can set your relationship with our generous Father on firm footing. Is there one particular area where you sense you are weak or which has perplexed you? The way is open for you to break through. Continue the experiment; things clear up when you're *doing*, not just pondering.

I hope you're praying with more confidence now, and enjoying the interaction with the Almighty that healthy petition can create. Now you're ready to look at specific questions related to special kinds of petition.

Is an idol lurking behind
the God you petition?

CHAPTER SEVEN

Asking the Right God for the Right Thing

SOME YEARS AGO Dr. William Parker invited forty-five people to participate in an unusual prayer experiment at the University of Redlands.[1] Each person had a definite physical, emotional, or spiritual need and a desire to find a solution. Many suffered from bodily ailments caused by stress; some were on the verge of acute nervous breakdown.

Dr. Parker divided the forty-five into three different groups, principally according to their preference. The fifteen who joined the "psychotherapy group" agreed to weekly individual counseling sessions. The fifteen in the "random prayer group" believed in the efficacy of prayer alone and agreed to pray about their problem every night before retiring. The fifteen in the "prayer therapy group" agreed to meet weekly for a two-hour session in which Parker would teach them to combine psychological insights with honest, positive prayer focused on God's healing love.

At the end of nine months all the participants were given standard Rorscharch, Szondi, and TAT tests to determine their attitudes, feelings, and adjustments. According to test results, 65 percent of those in psychotherapy showed improvement. Those in prayer therapy did even better:

72 percent showed evidence of positive change. But most surprising of all, those in the random prayer group showed no improvement at all.

Why these results? One can find ways to fault this experiment, pointing out that the test measure of results was biased toward psychological adjustment as opposed to spiritual growth, and that a zero rate of improvement is hard to believe even for people who do absolutely nothing. However, in examining the case studies that Dr. Parker presented, I was struck by the fact that those in prayer therapy learned to pray in a healthy way—and got results; while those in the random prayer group seemed stuck in unhealthy ways of petitioning—and remained stuck in their problems.

Jerry was a handsome, red-headed man of twenty-two who, except for a perpetual frown, seemed quite healthy. However, he'd convinced himself that he was a misfit who couldn't relate to other people. He'd failed to finish college, couldn't stick to one job, was depressed, nervous, and subject to frequent headaches. Jerry continued to depend on his parents financially and quarreled violently with them a great deal.

He wanted to join the random prayer group, explaining, "I've never prayed specifically about my problem, but I know if I do, it'll be answered. Being part of the experiment will help me to do it faithfully each night."

After testing Jerry, Dr. Parker and his associates concluded that he manifested a decided "will to failure." The young man was telling himself that if he really wanted to, or if other people were different, or if his family would leave him alone, then he could do great things. According to Dr. Parker, his continual failure spared him from having to exert the effort and self-discipline necessary to genuine success and also freed him from the potential shame of missing the mark should an honest endeavor fail. Although comforted and taken care of by his family, Jerry retained a deep hostility and guilt over the unacknowledged fact that he wasn't succeeding as he thought he should.

Jerry prayed every night for nine months. He employed a rote prayer for the most part, verbalizing his guilt and "wormy" feelings, constantly asking for forgiveness (and never taking it). For 271 evenings he reiterated his symptoms and his unworthiness to a remote God he wasn't sure was listening. Nothing much changed. He continued to be an ineffective person, plagued by headaches, constantly quarreling with his parents and the world.

Jerry's psychological counterpart in the experiment was Reverend G., a sixty-year-old Protestant minister with three grown daughters. Though intellectually brilliant, he'd played second fiddle to various other pastors his entire life and had been unable to win much confidence, friendship, or love from any congregation. Reverend G. admitted he was a failure, yet had an aura of condescension about him and spoke in critical, exacting tones. When this man joined the prayer therapy group, he said, "I have been praying for years. There must be either more to prayer than I know about, or much less than I've always hoped."

Psychological tests revealed a man who coupled high intellectual attainment with a total lack of emotional belief or conviction. Like Jerry, he possessed a will to fail. Afraid of God and unable to believe in himself, he was tormented by the anxiety and guilt of a person who preaches what he doesn't really understand or believe. Reverend G. felt a need to control every situation and yet couldn't relate to people well, being unaware of their needs.

When these facts came up in prayer therapy, Reverend G. found it difficult to accept them. The crowning blow was a slip of paper given to him, which stated bluntly that he needed "to be convinced of salvation through Christ," if he was ever to preach it successfully. This shook him and forced him into prayerful soul-searching. He admitted that he feared God, then chose the verse "Acquaint now thyself with me and be at peace" as his homework, and honestly sought in prayer to know what the heavenly Father was really like. When he finally opened himself to a God of love, improvement came rapidly. He quit trying to run the whole show, let God express Himself through others, and at last got a church of his own.

THE RIGHT GOD

Dr. Parker found that people learned to pray to the right God in several ways. Some participants experienced the Father's love by simply trying to love Him. Reverend G., for example, began admitting to God in prayer that he'd been kidding himself about their relationship. He said that he *did* want to believe in, trust, and love God and asked for His help. He began consciously to affirm throughout the day his budding love for and trust in a heavenly Father.

Still others absorbed the concept of a God of love by endeavoring to act lovingly toward those around them. A hypercritical woman named Sarah explained, "I couldn't love on order, but I could pray to be made more loving and then act as if this prayer had been granted." Gradually her conscious, willful acts of love, carried out in spite of her feelings, became genuine responses. She'd joined the group hoping that prayer power might change other people's lives. Instead, as Parker put it, "She found love changing her life and everyone around her reflecting that change." The woman's daughter-in-law came to visit one day just to see the class that had "worked miracles for Mother."

Other participants simply opened up to a new picture of a loving Father. A young man named Tony suffered from deep feelings of inferiority and had been afflicted with an agonizing stutter since childhood. Only in singing his favorite Brahms melodies could he escape the handicap. But one day the good news about a loving Father broke through: "After my morning prayer time, I had a sudden conviction that God wrote both Brahms and me. If God valued me enough to create me, He loved me. *God* loved *me!*" Group members noted a marked change in the young man's attitude, and he was able to overcome his stuttering.

All these people could probably have prayed obsessively about their problems with little result. Why? Because they needed to pray to the right God first. That was the key to their healing.

If your prayers about some problem consistently hit a brick wall, ask yourself if you're praying to the right God. Your rut may be trying to tell you something. Have you really accepted Christ's love for you personally?

If you approach the Lord with unresolved fear and hostility, a positive response on His part will tend to reinforce those attitudes. It's very important to God that you come to Him in response to His love. If you have negative feelings about Him because of some past experience, tell Him about it. Opening up candidly before the Father is the first step toward accepting His graciousness.

▼

THE RIGHT THING

One of those who participated in Dr. William Parker's prayer experiment was a deeply religious, forty-year-old woman who chose "prayer therapy" because her physicians and her spiritual advisor had all but given up hope of helping her overcome alcoholism. Various psychological tests pointed to deep-seated feelings of resentment, self-pity, guilt, and inferiority. According to Parker, all this created "a staggering burden separating her from any awareness of Love's healing power."

The woman couldn't understand why her desperate prayers to stop drinking hadn't been answered. She showed little interest in dealing with her emotional problems: "I want to stop drinking first. If I can't stop that, what does it matter? Why doesn't God help me?"

The answer dawned during an assignment to study the account in John 5 of Jesus healing the paralytic. The question, "Do you want to get well?" opened her eyes. She realized that in her heart of hearts she was not willing to be made

And please Lord, do something about Nancy.
She's always **SO** negative.

Don't just point out...when God wants you pointing in.

whole – only sober. She wanted to get rid of the pain of booze, a symptom, yet cling to her resentment, self-pity, etc. The woman came to acknowledge that she drank not because her husband's small income and her troublesome children made her life limited and mean, but because her attitude toward life was limited and mean.

So she surrendered these problems to God in prayer and took aim at different answers: loyalty, self-sacrifice, forgiveness. Dr. Parker witnessed her life changing dramatically as healing power was released.

This religious woman had banged away at the bottle in prayer with great earnestness – and in vain. Why? Because God wanted her to deal with a more fundamental problem: He wanted her to pray for the right thing.

If you've pounded on the door of mercy for some time with little or nothing to show for it, make sure you're not aiming at the wrong thing. Are you zeroed in on some symptom when you should be dealing with the moral disease itself? Are you ignoring the real solution?

At one time Dwight L. Moody could boast the largest Sabbath school and congregation in all Chicago and thought he was doing extremely well in the ministry. Like any pastor, he prayed for more growth. Two women who attended his meetings, however, suggested he pray for something else: power. Moody allowed that he had quite enough, thank you, judging by his accomplishments.

The women persisted, however, and finally Moody consented to pray with them for the "anointing of the Holy Ghost." A time of intense prayer created a new, ravenous hunger inside the man, which climaxed in a powerful encounter: "God revealed Himself to me, and I had such an experience of His love that I had to ask Him to stay His hand."

Moody did find spiritual power, something he had not thought to ask for or seek before. "I went on preaching again," he reported. "The sermons were not different; and I did not present any new truths, and yet hundreds were converted. I would not be placed back where I was before that blessed experience if you would give me all Glasgow."

Sometimes we miss the mark in prayer because our goals remain confined within the boundaries of personal desire. God certainly wants to meet our needs, spiritual and physical, but He doesn't want us to get stuck in the material world. James explained, "You do not have, because you do not ask God. When you ask, you do not receive, because you ask with wrong motives, that you may spend what you get on your pleasures" (4:2-3). If your petitions keep missing the mark, make sure your picture of life's necessities and God's picture of life's necessities are not miles apart.

Perhaps the most frequent way we aim at the wrong thing is this: asking God to change someone else or some situation when He wants to change us. We get stuck in a rut, hammering away at that outer impediment, when God is trying to get us to look at the snag within.

Something about our spouse may drive us up the wall. A coworker may irritate us beyond belief. So we pray. If only God would change so-and-so, life would be great. Of course, no one should tolerate physical or emotional abuse. But if it's a matter of Uncle Harry's forgetfulness, or your spouse leaving socks in the living room, and it ruins your whole day, take a look inside. Usually the things that bug us the most point to something within that needs fixing. Changing other people, more often than not, begins with God changing us.

I'm the kind of person who generally tries to bull through obstacles instead of waiting or finding a way around them. So sometimes my earnest requests to achieve a goal can simply be another method of stubbornly banging away. God is not likely to reinforce that disposition.

Every once in a while, however, God's alternative gets through. Once while making a film for a college class, I carefully set up a scene with a friend playing his guitar in an art gallery. Just as we were ready to roll, the camera light went out. After all that work I couldn't do a thing. I must have had a great quiet time that day because, instead of going through my usual operatic ranting, I suddenly wondered if the Lord wanted me to do something else. Could He use me in some other way? After packing away my equipment, I walked through the dorm and found a friend named Dave hovered over his study desk, something he was not accustomed to doing. Dave, I discovered, had been struggling to finish a term paper and couldn't get past a couple of knotted paragraphs. Being a communications major, I was able to help him untie a few sentences. He quickly completed the project, with corrections, much to his delight.

I am not naturally a helpful person, but I started to get the point. A few days later I was all set up to do some editing; several rolls of film were due. But they didn't come in. *Groan.* Well, maybe God had something else in mind. I ran into an acquaintance named Joe at the reception desk in the dorm lobby. He was excited about some package he'd been sent. When I offered to go with him to get it (having nothing else to do), Joe's face lit up, "Oh boy, I was hoping I'd have company." This kid proved to be an emotional disaster struggling to survive on campus, and I was able to offer him friendship. I got the point again.

We don't change overnight. I still sometimes kick angrily at temporary obstacles instead of looking for alternatives. But at least I know a little about praying for the right thing. I am less likely now to get fixated on praying for result X to happen NOW, placing God in a bind because He can't reward my impatience. I'm more likely to pray a much more answerable prayer, "Lord, show me what other good thing You have in mind."

Prayer Chain:
It's the <u>connection</u> that counts.

CHAPTER EIGHT

Praying by the Numbers

EVERY THURSDAY AT the offices of the television ministry I worked for, we brought in a box of letters containing prayer requests from our viewers. Passing around the slips of paper—often marked in the large, uncertain scrawl of the elderly—we read what was on people's hearts. Those were sobering bits of literature; a few pleading lines opened a view of a world plagued by unfaithful spouses, drug-abusing children, incurable illnesses, and scheming in-laws.

Those earnest people wanted us to intercede on their behalf, or more specifically, they hoped our avuncular speaker who appeared on the screen each week would pray for them. Staff members, led by the speaker, dutifully summarized the requests and lifted them up to the throne of grace. But sometimes while kneeling I wondered just exactly what we were doing for these strangers.

Were we adding to the number of human voices raising a certain petition up to the Almighty and thus persuading Him to do something by acclamation? Were we in that religious ministry expected to have an inside track to the ear of the Lord? Or did the godly gentleman, the pastor, by his endorsement help petitions get through to the top?

All of us, at some time or another, wonder: Do numbers help when it comes to petition? Are they an extra shove for our most desperate pleas?

MECHANICS VERSUS INVOLVEMENT

What does the Bible say about praying by the numbers? The first text that comes to mind is Matthew 18:19-20: "I tell you that if two of you on earth agree about anything you ask for, it will be done for you by my Father in heaven. For where two or three come together in my name, there am I with them."

Some people, looking at such a promise, conclude that if two are good, four must be even better. If two people agreeing in petition are granted such power, they say, imagine what twenty or four hundred could accomplish! We can slip into a mechanistic approach to prayer that echoes pagans chanting endlessly to their gods. Jesus discouraged attempts to gain a heavenly hearing by the sheer length of one's prayers; the same must hold for sheer numbers. God is not compelled to do by acclamation what He refuses to do for the lone petitioner.

The promise about two or three gathered in Christ's name is best understood in company with the promise about the mustard seed. The point being that even a bit of faith, a mustard seed worth of sincere belief, is capable of working wonders. The point here is that even two or three gathered in Christ's name are enough to gain a hearing—that's all it takes.

But just as we accept this word of caution we run into verses in the New Testament epistles that seem to call for more numbers, more petitioners. The Apostle Paul's appeals are unmistakable. He wants the believers in Rome praying for him: "I urge you . . . to join me in my struggle by praying to God for me." He wants the Corinthians to petition: "You also joining in helping us through your prayers." The apostle

covets Ephesian prayer: "Pray also for me . . . that I will fear-
lessly make known the mystery of the gospel."[1]

That's quite a lot of people. Was the apostle turning his
requests before God into a sure thing by such wide and persistent backing?

If we look at these appeals carefully, two things become
evident: the involvement of those asked to pray, and the confidence of the one asking. The believers in Rome, Corinth,
and Ephesus were deeply bonded to Paul; they weren't praying for a stranger. Many of them dated their spiritual birth to
some testimony for Christ Paul gave at the dock or market
or jail. And they were also bound in ministry with Paul; his
work in spreading the gospel was their work; his struggles
against opposition were their struggles. They prayed as participants in the same movement; their hearts beat with his
same passion.

This leads us to suggest a guideline for making prayer
more answerable: The more involved a petitioner is with the
person or problem prayed for, the more significant his or her
role as an intercessor before God. This does not mean, of
course, that it is wrong to pray for strangers, but that we
are most powerful in prayer when we don't pray from the
sidelines.

The second element we can see in Paul's appeals for
prayer is his cheery confidence. We don't find a man franti-
cally gathering prayer support, like some candidate hustling
votes at a political convention, because he is so fearful of
not getting what he asks for. On the contrary, the remarkable thing is that Paul seems to request prayer precisely
because he is sure it will be answered in a certain way. He
asks the Corinthian believers to pray "that thanks may be
given by many persons on our behalf for the favor bestowed"
(2 Corinthians 1:11, NASB). The more people who pray, the
more who will then be able to rejoice personally in the answer
given.

So, to make your requests more answerable, ask others
to pray in a spirit of confidence, with a desire that they share

in the happiness of the answer. You want those involved in some way in your life or in the matter you're praying for to turn their concern into specific petition.

Soon after coming to a Presbyterian church in a small Midwestern town, a young, timid pastor found himself at odds with the leading elder who functioned like a political boss. Unable and unwilling to outfight such an expert opponent, the pastor resigned and left.

Two years later he was recalled to the same congregation—and faced the same elder, who was being charged with financial misconduct. Fortunately, the presbytery managed to depose the man. However, he purchased space in the local newspaper, pouring slanderous abuse on the church and its members in an effort to vindicate himself. This went on for weeks until the ex-elder closed with a challenge: "Put this matter to a test! You Presbyterians are praying for a revival. If revival comes, you are proved right, and I wrong. If not, I am right and you wrong, as I have said. 'Shall not the Judge of the earth do right?'"

This rather feeble congregation had before prayed for renewal only in the vaguest terms. In fact, they had no experience whatever of revival in the usual sense of the term. But now, pastor and people began petitioning earnestly in preparation for their annual "week of prayer." They were all very much involved; their part of the Body of Christ was placed under a glaring spotlight.

On Sunday, the first night of the meetings, the church was filled "beyond any precedent for evening service in that church, or in the experience of that pastor." The usual gathering of elderly women was wonderfully augmented by a strong male showing.

In the front row sat a bootlegger who was popularly designated "the wickedest man in town." During the second service this man stood and announced his intention of living a Christian life. By Saturday night, fifteen people had added their affirmations to his. The week of prayer extended two more weeks, during which fourteen more people found their way to Christ. No one in that quiet town had ever seen so "sudden and decisive a work of grace."[2]

▼

PRIVATE DESIRES VERSUS MUTUAL WISDOM

During a weekly time of prayer, several missionaries began to talk about their present needs and make prayer requests. When Bob's turn came, his puffy cheeks, red eyes, and constant use of a handkerchief made it obvious what he needed. "I can't seem to shake this cold," he said quietly. "It just keeps hanging on. I'd like you to pray that I'll be able to get rid of it."

They all nodded politely, all except for the man's secretary, Lucille, a woman with soft gray hair and an angelic face. She said firmly, "Sorry. I'm not going to pray for you, Bob."

The rest of the group looked at her in amazement. She continued, "You've been staying at the office every night until ten with hardly a break for meals. You're working yourself to death. Now you want God to heal you. I don't think He will, and I'm not going to pray about it."

Lucille had such an impish look in her eyes as she spoke that the rest, including Bob, couldn't help chuckling. The overworked man meekly promised to reform his lifestyle immediately, and Lucille consented to pray.

If Bob's request had remained purely private, he could have much more easily gone on petitioning God for health and working himself to death. But fortunately there was another believer there to jolt him awake.

One-to-one communication with God will always remain the heart and soul of prayer, but group petition serves as an important balancing element that sharpens our aim and keeps us on track of more answerable petitions.

William Parker's prayer experiment made clear that some people can get into unhealthy ruts as they wage lone combat on their knees. Without feedback from other believers, a person's quirks, pettinesses, or obsessive tendencies

Praying in harmony
helps us hit the right note.

can get him stuck in a negative pounding on the door of mercy. Our Lord has advised us to send up petitions together for the same reason He urges us not to forsake assembling together to worship.

Selfish or wrong-headed prayers that are easy to repeat in private don't sound the same before fellow believers. We simply aim better when two or three are agreed on a certain petition. Openly talking about our goals creates more room in which wisdom can stake its claims.

INTERDEPENDENCE VERSUS BUREAUCRACY

First Corinthians 12 makes plain that Christ has designed the Church, His Body on earth, to perform better as an interdependent system than as a series of freelancing organs. We witness separately, but our witness is magnified when we speak together. We worship on our own, but our worship has special power when we praise God together. We give as individuals, but our giving accomplishes much more when pooled.

Prayer is a part of that, a part of the dynamics of Christ's Body. We accomplish far more together than apart. But it's important to regard this prayer system as a network and *not* as a bureaucracy.

In medieval times the church developed an elaborate hierarchy through which the average believer had to approach God. Jesus, often pictured as the fiery King coming to judge the earth, required the softening touch of the virgin Mary; it became easier to pray to the awesome Son through this tender mother. But soon the church had magnified Mary's sanctity to such mythical proportions that she seemed out of reach. Martyrs and saints began to appear a bit more accessible; if you could win a hearing through one of them, especially your own personal saint, they would be able to appeal to Mary, Mary to Jesus, and Jesus to the inscrutable Father. And finally, it was best to start the whole process through the mediation of your neighborhood priest.

Protestants and many Catholics today decry a system like this, which inserts so many obstacles between God and the individual. Most of us think of it as a relic of the superstitious past. Yet the ghost of that bureaucracy still haunts us, exploiting our elemental need to be worthy, to make sure. We still subconsciously want to go through someone to God; we tend to believe that some distant, celebrity minister's petition will carry more to recommend it than our own. We seek to claim a special hearing through those we perceive as God's closer associates.

Again, asking others to intercede for us is not wrong. It's why and how we do it that makes the difference. Are we networking or going through a bureaucracy? Nothing should overshadow the fact that each of us as sinners clinging to Christ are given *carte blanche* to come boldly before the throne of grace and present our petitions. When we pray together we need to see ourselves as one body functioning together, not as layers of saints funneling pleas up to the most godly among us.

In my experience, prayer groups wield petition to great effect—no matter who the participants are. Various dynamics of the Spirit come into play. People usually get more serious, more earnest, about their requests when petition becomes a shared exercise. Something greater is created than the sum of each petition.

Confessing a need or a desire before fellow believers seems to concentrate spiritual power. We stake a public claim to God's intervention, activating our faith. This must have a positive effect similar to that of confessing the name of Christ before others. It's healthy, and God is eager to reinforce the healthy functioning of His Body. Again, the quantity of prayers stacking up toward Heaven is not what makes the difference, but the quality of concerned, involved people gathered in Christ's name. When believers act unitedly, the Spirit's potential power becomes kinetic energy.

A certain clergyman once attempted to comfort a woman mourning the fact that her husband, a bitter agnostic, had left town during a revival, determined not to return "till the religious flurry is over." The wife had been hoping and praying that he would be converted, but now there seemed little chance. On hearing the story, the pastor decided to take this opportunity to "lay his case before the Lord, and make special request that God will bring him back again under the power of the Spirit." The minister invited her to attend the morning prayer group he was about to lead.

Seizing this ray of hope, the woman dried her tears and accompanied him to the home where parishioners gathered for prayer. The room was full that day as the pastor presented the case of the "Universalist husband" and appealed for united petition that the man be overtaken, brought back, shown his sins, and led to Christ. The believers immediately took the challenge with such earnestness that, as the pastor recalled, "I could not but feel that prayer would in some way be answered."

That same night the fugitive astounded everyone by showing up at the evening meeting and telling his story. He'd ridden eighteen miles into the hills when he was stopped in his tracks, he said, "as Paul was, and just as suddenly, and made to feel what a horrible sinner I am. . . . I now know that I must be born again, or I can never see the kingdom of Heaven."[3] The unmistakably retrieved gentleman took his seat amid the tears and sobs of the whole congregation.

Look for a pattern
in your answers to prayer.

CHAPTER NINE

Tracking Answers

THE DIARIES OF the New England Puritan Cotton Mather are remarkable in part because they record a life both deeply pious and keenly analytical. One of the things the Reverend Mather noted with great care was his experience with "Particular Faith." This involved vivid assurances of what God intended to do, sometimes in direct response to prayer. One day while he was pondering his lack of money to buy a new cloak, Mather received an assurance that he would never want proper clothing. "Immediately after these Thoughts" a parishioner surprised him with a present of a "handsome and costly cloak."

Cotton Mather came to define particular faith as "a little degree of the Spirit of Prophecy," which assured the petitioner that a certain prayer would be answered. It seems to have been something stronger than the usual assurance of faith: "This persuasion, is not a mere Notion, and Fancy, but a Special Impression from Heaven," striking with a "powerful, Heart melting, Heavenly Afflatus."

When his daughter Nancy became quite ill with intense stomach pains, Mather, in his fervent prayers on her behalf, became "Irradiated from Heaven with a Particular Faith, for

some Help to be sent from Heaven unto the dying Child."
The girl began vomiting and a physician concluded she was
about to perish. However, Nancy didn't. Several days later
she began "running and laughing the whole Forenoon, about
the House," and soon recovered fully.

During the long series of European conflicts that followed
King William's accession in 1689, Mather's millennial expectations were aroused. He received "a strong Persuasion, that
some very overturning Dispensations of Heaven, will quickly
befall the French Empire." And he prayed fervently for the
fulfillment of these intimations, believing that secret prayer
does "an incredible deal, towards Jogging the High Wheels of
Providence,and Shaking of Churches, and Empires." He saw
"astonishing Answers" to petition in the revival of Protestant-
ism in Orange, "the Bowels of France," and expressed thanks
to Christ for having "informed, inclined, and assisted . . . a
vile Sinner, in a Corner of America, to foresee, and put on
that Work of His."[1]

MOVABLE AND IMMOVABLE TARGETS

Cotton Mather is among the many prayer veterans who
seem to have attained an assurance, on occasion, that
their prayers will be answered. Not all such petitioners use
the same language. Some talk of "praying through" the problem until some assurance is achieved. Others stake absolute
claim on certain surefire scriptural promises. But all appear
to experience a certainty that eludes the rest of us.

Is particular faith for everybody? Can we ever know for
sure that our target is certain? Is there such a thing as certainty in prayer?

First, we should acknowledge that there are immov-
able targets, things we won't ever miss. It is *always* God's
will to pardon those who sincerely and repentantly seek it.
There are no exceptions. It is *always* God's desire to give
us the Holy Spirit, the ability to witness and love. There
are no conceivable circumstances in which God would not

want to bestow these gifts. We need to ask for, believe, and receive them.

Other requests are open-ended, because God's will is more open-ended at certain points. The particular assurances we need involve moving targets: petitions we aim into the web of circumstances surrounding our lives, requests we attempt to sync up with the specific how, when, where, and who of God's will.

GET THE FACTS

The best way to develop such assurances is to do what I call "prayer tracking." Begin to keep a record of your specific prayer requests and exactly what happens as a result. Get down as much information as you can: what exactly you request, how you pray, what promises you claim, when you petition, and any subsequent events that seem relevant. This requires, of course, that you pray about a variety of things over a period of time. Sporadic requests don't give you much feedback. You want to develop a prayer history so you can relate to a pattern of divine responses rather than to occasional vague impressions or sharp disappointments.

Tracking will also help you spot any number of factors (as covered in previous chapters) that make petitions more answerable. If you're not really aiming, that will become apparent immediately. If you're generally passive in prayer or aim only at long-term goals, that too will become evident. As you conscientiously note the condition in which you pray, any sin problems that are jamming the works should surface. The practice of tracking itself will help you pray more deliberately, since you're writing something down, keeping an eye out for a divine response. Persistence in the request follows more naturally.

Tracking also helps you see answers to prayer that otherwise could drift by without notice. I have a feeling that we miss a lot of what God is doing because we aren't paying attention.

If it weren't for a small note at the bottom of a page in my prayer journal, I may not have realized how providential a certain encounter in my college dorm was. I had run into a shy freshman named Sean and invited him to a Bible study prayer group. After I got to know him a bit, he revealed that he was struggling with homosexual feelings. He also told me his father had threatened to kill him if he ever found him "doing that stuff again." Sean said he'd thought of doing away with himself.

Then the lights went on. Shortly before meeting Sean, we'd been talking in our prayer group about the shocking news that a few of our fellow students had attempted suicide. As a result, we'd begun to pray earnestly, "Lord, lead us to one." God did, and we were able to offer Sean some much-needed support.

That encounter still encourages me. I see the providential connection because I got it down in black and white. Without the attention of tracking, the event probably would have faded into the undecipherable past by now.

Beyond helping us see *more* providences, tracking enables us to search for some pattern. If you're just starting to keep a prayer diary, begin with a retroactive approach to tracking: Look back through your life as a believer and try to reconstruct your prayer history. When, how, and under what circumstances have you seen your prayers answered? What did God do specifically? What can you learn from the way He responded?

The tracking process is especially useful as we attempt to interpret the results of our petitions. Let's say you pray earnestly about being able to help grumpy Aunt Zelda get along with the family. But in your next encounter you have a big fight. Is God saying, "I want you to pray in a different direction," or is He telling you, "Redouble your efforts"? In many different situations a problem can be seen either as the Devil throwing up a roadblock or as the Lord sending us on a detour.

In an isolated incident, making out any clear divine signal is difficult. But if you have been keeping track of

your prayers and their results, you'll have more information on which to base your response. For example, if praying
about problem X usually gets you nowhere, then a different
direction is in order—a different goal or type of prayer. Perhaps you need to listen and think seriously about asking the
right God for the right thing. But if you have seen results in
the past when attacking one kind of problem in prayer, then
you should probably "pray through." You can be more confident about redoubling your efforts when roadblocks appear.
Reviewing similar petitions and similar circumstances helps
you decipher an intelligible sentence out of God's running
dialogue.

▼

OUR PRAYER GIFT

A satyrical English clergyman named Swift once announced
from the pulpit, "My brethren, there are three kinds of pride—
of birth, of riches, and of talent. I shall not speak of the latter,
none of you being liable to that abominable vice."

Today most ministers know better than to make that
assumption, even in jest. According to Christ's parable, all of
us are given at least one talent. And according to the epistles,
everyone in Christ's Body has a special gift.

Tracking can help us find out about our individual prayer
gift. I believe there's an area of prayer or a kind of prayer in
which each of us is gifted and in which we may develop a
high degree of assurance. It's often affirmed that all those "in
Christ" possess various gifts of the Spirit—teaching, exhortation, healing, administration—which indicate in what area
we may most profitably function for the Lord. We are frequently advised to discover what our gift is, so that we can
focus our energies more effectively. Believers talk about a
variety of gifts and ministries in the Body of Christ even though
all of us have equal access to the power of God, an equal share
in the indwelling Spirit, and the same designation as children
of God, servants of Christ, disciples, and ambassadors.

You'll go farther if
you go where you're gifted.

We can look at prayer in a similar way. We may each have a particular area of prayer in which we are most effective, even though all of us have equal access to God's throne, all of us are recipients of "marvelous promises," and all of us can do more than we imagine through prayer. Perhaps there are special targets at which you are called to aim.

If you find that you have consistent success in praying for a certain thing, that topic of petition could be part of your prayer gift. In looking back over my own prayer history, I invariably pick up one bright spot: praying about people I don't like.

During college I developed a supportive closeness with five other guys in a Christian group on campus. But one evening a six-foot-five football player burst into our quiet gathering, extended his hand in all directions, and bellowed out his name. Big Wally, I discovered, was the latest addition to our group. For me the spell was broken; I was sure our tranquil, reflective meetings would never be the same.

As I listened to Wally's opinions boom across the room during subsequent sessions, I realized that, not only were our personalities poles apart, some of his all-American religious views were those I disdained.

Fortunately, our group leader came up with a new way to open our fellowship time. He asked us to pray silently for each group member, thinking of their needs and claiming God's assistance in their lives. I prayed for the person on my right, on my left, then came to Wally, sitting across the room. Somehow I could no longer think of him in the same way. He required my help, and I, his.

The more we prayed together, the more I saw things to admire in this effusive jock. One evening I found myself jumping on a sofa, wildly celebrating an answer to prayer with Wally. His raw enthusiasm had become infectious rather than offensive.

A certain student missionary named Fred also comes to mind. I worked and lived with him in Japan, and he started getting on my nerves. Fred loved to shop; all he seemed to talk about were cameras, stereos, and clothes. I was into roughing it as a missionary, doing without. Fred was too inhibited to join us at the public (though gender-segregated) bath. He insisted on conversing at 2:00 a.m. My list of things to dislike grew longer.

One day we caught the same commuter train into Osaka. And we started talking. I found out he was struggling to establish good devotional habits. I was too. We decided we'd both study the book of Galatians each morning.

A week later we got together and shared what we learned. It proved enlightening for both of us. Those first verses of Galatians about Jesus Christ rescuing us from this present evil age came alive. I was amazed at how much this one mutually exciting activity awakened my sympathies for Fred. He wasn't just a consumer freak anymore. We still had our differences, but God was with us. We had that common ground. It had been there all along, but unacknowledged.

There have been other occasions, involving other people, when God nudged me into a new perspective, sometimes hitting me between the eyes. Looking back on those events I naturally have a great deal of confidence now in praying about people who rub me the wrong way. It's a kind of assurance or "intimation" based on what God has done in the past.

It's good to know our strengths, as well as our weaknesses, in the Christian life. When we restrict our petitions to hammering away at some obstacle, inside or out, the rest of our spiritual life often stalls. We keep waiting for the break-through. But when we're able to focus on one area where we're experiencing positive change, this tends to pull other facets of growth along with it.

Growing into an assurance about our petitions can start with confidence in a certain topic of prayer. And this area of success can gradually expand. My prayer life didn't end with casting about for potential enemies. I moved from there to praying about being more encouraging and asking God to bless specific people in various ways through my efforts.

We continue to pray about all kinds of things, of course. But we can decide to major in a certain area of prayer. Just as there are pastors, teachers, and administrators who expand God's work in various spheres, so there can be prayer warriors who are equipped to extend His providence into certain areas of life.

Above all, don't let the idea of a prayer gift become restrictive. It is best used as a door into more answerable prayer, a way to build your assurance about what God will do. Healthy prayer is always expansive; it leads us steadily into the wideness and depth of our heavenly Father's world.

PROVIDENTIAL MOMENTUM

Early in her career, Amy Carmichael, the luminous missionary Elizabeth Elliot describes in *A Chance to Die*,[2] attempted to teach Japanese villagers about Christ. She made plans to visit the town of Hirosi, where only eight or nine Christians could be located. Amy wanted very much to know what God intended to do there and spent time in prayer, attempting to find the target that she should seize by faith.

An answer came: Amy felt "pressed in spirit" to ask the Master for one convert, and did so. The next day she visited Hirosi with her Japanese companion and conducted an evening meeting. A young silk weaver "crossed the line" into faith. A month later Amy went again, this time impressed to ask for two souls. A friend of the silk weaver who came to listen "found peace," and an elderly woman also placed her faith in Christ.

Two weeks later it was time for another visit, and Amy again asked God what He wanted to do. Win four more, was the answer. So she claimed four in prayer. Her missionary colleagues grew worried: "You can't expect conversions every time." Asking for four souls seemed a bit much; nobody else in the town seemed in the least interested. Amy's outreach was greatly complicated at this point by her conviction that she should tell new converts to burn their idols. This, others assured her, would turn away all inquirers. But Amy resolved not to "buy a soul at the cost of sacrificing truth."

At the next meeting her listeners stared back politely and dully; nothing seemed to get through. But just before Amy closed the service a woman said, "I want to believe." Then her son came up and knelt beside her. On the way home Amy stopped at the house of believers; a friend of theirs was waiting to ask her about the way to salvation. Number three. What about the fourth? "It must be my wife," a man offered. "She wants to be a Jesus-person, but she is away at her own village." Early the next morning this woman returned and confessed her desire to be a Christian.

In the following weeks, Amy was moved to ask for eight converts from Hirosi. Her colleagues balked again. She offered to stay longer during the next visit and conduct more meetings. The other missionaries assured her that this could not possibly be arranged. But concluding somewhat nervously that God had been speaking to her, they agreed to ask and believe. After the next visit, eight more "stars" in Hirosi shone brightly in the night.

What was next on God's agenda? Sixteen? This time no number at all was laid on Amy's heart in prayer. She went without making specific claims to the Father, had the usual meetings, and prayed with the Christians. Several people came to Christ. She was not sure exactly how many.

What strikes me most about this providential episode is that Amy Carmichael seemed to be in sync with divine momentum that carried her along with something approaching certainty. She was able to tap into a spurt of spiritual multiplication, but she didn't run the formula into the ground. There are times when answers to prayer flow thick and fast, or at least thicker and faster. One secret of making our petitions more answerable is knowing when to get on a roll and when to get off.

I experienced the beginning of a bit of that providential momentum the summer before my sophomore year in college. I had to decide between Western Illinois University and a Christian college in Michigan. Big things were happening at the Christian college; a revival had broken out the previous year. The university, by contrast, seemed a vast secular wasteland of anonymous learning. As I deliberated, my father mentioned off-hand the vast difference in tuition.

I decided to pray about my decision for several days. It was the first time I had considered God as a viable factor in decision making. Would He show me which way was best? At the end of a series of prayer sessions, a clear idea had developed: I basically wanted to go to Michigan for the social life and that wasn't a good enough reason to cost my parents *beaucoup* bucks. So I resignedly enrolled at Western . . . and ran headlong into Campus Crusade for Christ, the greatest discipling experience of my life. Everything changed; I was catapulted into a dynamic spiritual movement.

Two years later I faced the same decision: Should I take my senior year at the Christian college in Michigan or stay at Western? I had to think about where to get lined up with a career. After much prayer, and a financial break, God seemed to be pointing to Michigan. I was a bit resigned this time also, believing that I was going to a denominational ghetto. But surprisingly enough God opened up ways for me to keep expanding, even there—principally through a prison ministry.

Next I had to decide what to do after college. More prayer. I became a missionary to Japan, teaching English and Bible. Outreach expanded exponentially. I was working with people who had little idea who God was, much less what the good news about Jesus was all about.

At the end of my one-year term I faced a difficult choice: (A) Go back to the States and start a career (get a real job, as they say); (B) stay another year in Japan. The factors bearing on the two alternatives were complex and for the most part unknowable. I prayed more earnestly than ever, wanting very much for God to speak up loud and clear. Nothing audible happened, but certain factors came to the fore: I knew people who had no contact with Christianity besides myself and who were still in spiritual limbo; I didn't want to end those relationships.

So I chose to stay on, and feeling bullish about these "impressions," I thanked God ahead of time for the new growth in outreach He would initiate—even though I would be assigned the same tasks the second year. I could see we were on a roll in this area. Every new step He'd guided me through had led to a definite expansion of ministry.

At the beginning of the second term, the school director invited me into his office and popped one of the most wonderful questions I'd heard in my life: Would I be interested in making films for his evangelistic meetings? I was elated. Making movies had always been my big, long-term dream. But here, where I least expected it, God dropped it right in my lap. And that new phase of ministry was precisely what I had thanked God for ahead of time. During the next year and a half I created a variety of films, from pantomime to documentary, on all kinds of themes. It was a rare creative opportunity.

I'll always cherish memories of that time in my life, where each divinely guided transition opened up a new exciting sphere of activity. But that momentum didn't last forever. After I married and moved to Southern California to do film work, there was no apparent great leap forward in outreach. I realized that God did not have a mechanical program functioning in perpetuity. A certain phase of God's plan had ended. It was time to look for the next one.

Each one of us will have chances to tap into the divine momentum. We need to be ready, waiting and listening. Tracking is part of that process. As we record our petitions and their results, we'll better know when we're on a certain roll with the Lord and when it's time to move on to something else. Our lives are more exciting than we think. God's momentum is nearer than we think. When He leaps forward, enjoy the ride with Him.

You can get lost
going too fast, going too slow.

CHAPTER TEN

When "Signs" Backfire

IT WAS TO BE A meeting with the Great Divine Will, something like Israel's high priest entering the holy place and getting a glow from either Urim or Thumim—yes or no. I needed to know whether I had to go knock on the neighbor's door and confess that I had broken a branch in his hedge while playing a vigorous game of capture-the-flag, or if I could just pass this off as no great transgression. I approached the quandary with all the anguished earnestness of an eleven-year-old seeking truth.

Walking slowly out of the house with a copy of the *Junior Guide*, a church publication for early-teens, I climbed a guava tree that overlooked the ominous, fractured hedge. Under a beaming blue sky, with only a light breeze ruffling the quiet of our yard, I asked God to show me clearly what I should do. I'd decided to open the *Junior Guide* at random, begin reading, and stop when I found either a "yes" or a "no" in the text. That would be the sign.

It was very important that God speak. My active conscience wouldn't let me rest until the matter was settled. So I solemnly opened the magazine and pored over a story, having figured that God could most readily guide me through a religious publication. Pretty soon I came across a stray "no." Terrific, God had answered; I was off the hook.

As I started climbing back down to earth, the drone of conscience picked up again. Maybe I should make sure. So I prayed again, pleading for another indication of that immutable will. I opened the magazine at random and began reading. This time, to my dismay, I came across a "yes" first.

It is difficult from this adult distance to sense what an impact that divine contradiction had on a religious kid. For a moment my world trembled on the edge of chaos. Was God really there? Did He communicate?

Subsequent experiments with prayer and the *Junior Guide* yielded the same ambiguous results. So I gave up on the guava tree and God speaking. For quite a few years afterward, this disappointment remained in the back of my mind as a mystifying strike against what I believed. Even after I'd matured to some extent and realized that there were better ways of seeking divine guidance, I still didn't understand why God hadn't met me on my level. I'd been so earnest.

Then something finally turned on the lights. I saw why the Father had been eager to nip my random yes-or-no test in the bud. This kind of compulsive reliance on signs was precisely what a hypersensitive boy didn't need. The best thing for me was to grow up and start using my mind, not run to some external trick every time I faced a dilemma.

If I had been honest I would have seen that my fervent searching was motivated by a desire to find a way out of a difficult situation. I didn't want to confront that neighbor. How nice it would have been to find a divine "no" to fall back on.

If there's one type of prayer that has been the most difficult for Christians to make more answerable, it's the prayer for divine guidance. Seeking God's will has acquired more than its share of pitfalls and dead ends. Yet it remains a great quest for believers. We hope that our all-knowing, loving heavenly Father will lead us to the perfect spouse, perfect job, and perfect home. We visualize God's will as a yellow brick road, steering us unerringly to that wonderful life just beyond the rainbow.

But many of us become disillusioned. God doesn't seem to speak as pointedly as we hoped. Sometimes what we see as "God opening a door" leads into a brick wall. Why do we end up on so many detours? Are we misreading the signs, is the yellow brick road overgrown with weeds, or is God simply not telling?

I believe two basic mistakes cause most of our perplexity when we pray for guidance.

IMPULSIVE RABBITS

Rick and Sandy enjoyed singing together. And their college classes weren't that meaningful for either of them. They began to sense that the Holy Spirit was calling them into a full-time music ministry. The signs seemed favorable. Rick and Sandy dropped out of school, got married, and sold everything they owned to buy sound equipment and a customized van.

Months later the two were bitterly accusing God of leading them astray. They had no singing engagements, were deeply in debt, and were expecting a baby. What had happened to that wonderful "calling"?

These two young people, no doubt, felt a strong pull toward a music ministry. They were bored with college; they longed to be married and independent. Urges that strong are easily interpreted as divine guidance. Unfortunately, Rick and Sandy ended up *running ahead* of God.

I call people who repeatedly make this mistake "impulsive rabbits." The rabbits among us tend to base major life decisions on subjective impressions. For them the statement, "I've been impressed to . . ." is sometimes only a religious-sounding version of "I feel like. . . ." They find themselves flitting here and there a lot, nose to the air, reacting to all kinds of stray scents.

When rabbits ask for signs to guide them, they're tempted

to stack the odds in their favor: a likely sign for yes, an improbable sign for no. For example they might pray, "If You don't want us to get married, Lord, then take away our love for each other completely." Or, "Lord, if You don't want me to make this trip, don't let the car start." The car has always started before. So it's very likely the person will go on his journey, assured of divine blessing.

When rabbits look to God's Word, their own desires again cloud the picture. They might choose to read in Psalms, for example. It's probable they will read something they interpret as positive or encouraging—an assurance of God's blessing, perhaps, or a command to persevere or go forward. This general encouragement is taken as a specific confirmation of their cherished plans, and impulsive rabbits step right out—ahead of God.

CAUTIOUS SLOTHS

Other people have a very different problem. Those I call "cautious sloths" are always seeking guidance, waiting for guidance, and never quite getting the right guidance. They're always hanging around, gazing toward the sky for something to drop down on them and, as a result, frequently lag behind God's will.

Sloths want to see some arbitrary, dramatic "sign" before acting. Rabbits make their "signs" too easy; sloths make them too difficult. Rabbits take off and keep going until a door slams in their face. Sloths want to see freeways stretch out before them. The latter tend to be fatalistic—whatever happens is God's will. Difficulties are not challenges to overcome, but divine placards announcing "turn back."

Cautious sloths typically yearn for "the peace of God" before making major decisions; their goal is complete assurance. They don't recognize that all big decisions make us nervous. It is unlikely, for example, that any groom has ever felt "the peace of God" right before his wedding. His palms are clammy, his throat dry. His whole life may be passing before him. That doesn't mean God is telling him not to go through with it. But in such situations, sloths are usually filled with misgivings.

A young opera student in Munich was practicing a role in the garden of his boarding house. He began singing the lines, "Come to me, my love, on the wings of light." Just then, to his utter amazement, a young lady dropped out of the sky and landed at his feet. His heavenly visitor turned out to be a Bavarian actress doing a stunt for a movie. She had parachuted from a plane right into his arms. As it turned out, in a few months the two were married—love did indeed come to the young student "on the wings of light."

That certainly was a remarkable encounter, but most of us realize that spouses don't normally drop from Heaven into our laps. Sloths, however, seem to wait for such an event to interrupt their plodding lives. And often they remain singing in the garden, longing for a role to play, but never getting the call.

Our first challenge as believers who want to zero in on the will of God is to avoid the mistakes of the rabbits and the sloths: running ahead of God and lagging behind Him. We need to find ways to walk more in step with the One whose will is good, acceptable, and perfect.

FACING THE RIGHT DIRECTION

While traveling by mule through the countryside of Spain, Ignatius of Loyola met a follower of Islam, a Moor. The two rode together awhile and struck up a conversation. The Moor soon learned that Ignatius was on his way to the Church of Our Lady of Montserrat, and he scoffed at the idea of penance before the virgin Mary. Ignatius quickly rebuked this "infidel" for his disrespect. The two argued back and forth, their exchanges becoming more and more heated, until the Moor spurred his mount and galloped ahead.

Ignatius was furious and felt a strong urge to go after the Moor and kill him. The man had told him where he would leave the highway and follow a trail to a certain village. As Ignatius approached this fork in the road, he couldn't decide what to do. He determined to let his mule act as a sign. He dropped the reins on its neck. If the animal followed the Moor's trail, he would kill him. If it stayed on the main road, he would let the man live. Fortunately, the mule kept to the easier highway.

In his struggle to make up his mind, Ignatius apparently forgot about God's moral will. The Father had been very clear about murder, and Jesus had been very clear about loving our neighbor. But instead of sticking to the center of divine precept, Ignatius let the mule decide.

To make our petitions for guidance more answerable it's best to first make sure we're facing in the right direction. Besides having specific plans for individuals, God has a common moral will that applies to everyone. In order to begin seeing down the road God has laid out for us, we must first stand firmly within His moral principles.

Some of us find ourselves constantly testing the boundaries of God's law, always asking, "Is this or that really wrong?" "Wouldn't it be okay if I just . . . ?" If we find ourselves frequently bumping into do's and don'ts, something may be wrong with our sense of direction. A lot of energy is wasted careening to the edges of the divine pathway.

It's very dangerous to seek signs or follow impressions that lead us over the edge of God's moral will—just this once, just in this special-case exemption from the rules. Scripture gives an abundance of clear, moral instruction on which to pattern our lives. All of us require that essential guidance.

One great thing about God's moral will is that it gives us both *limits* and the *freedom to act*. God wants us to be able to make choices comfortably within His moral will. For example, in the matter of offerings, Paul advised, "Each man should give what he has decided in his heart to give, not reluctantly or under compulsion, for God loves a cheerful giver" (2 Corinthians 9:7). Giving to those in need is part of

God's moral will. But how much? When? To whom? Generally speaking, we are to make those decisions freely and cheerfully, as we are moved in our hearts.

INDIVIDUAL PURPOSE

All of us are called to live within God's law, but we don't carry out His multifaceted purposes in the same way. Each of us possesses unique gifts and a special calling in life. So the next step in seeking guidance is to pray and think about what our central purpose is, as individuals. It helps to look at how we are gifted. The God of abundance has shared various talents, abilities, skills, and spiritual gifts with each of His children.

Romans 12, 1 Corinthians 12, and Ephesians 4 list gifts of the Spirit, such as teaching, giving, exhortation. That's a good place to start, but there are many other gifts. Ask yourself what gives you the most satisfaction. Do you have any persistent burdens or desires about a particular kind of work? Look at the results of your efforts. What are you good at? Also, ask trusted friends what they see as your gifts or abilities.

Paul understood clearly his basic purpose in life as an apostle to the Gentiles. He determined to preach the gospel where Christ was not yet known. This man's gifts and abilities qualified him for this special work. Paul had grown up in a Greek culture but also received the best rabbinical training, so he was able to bridge the gap between the Jewish and Gentile worlds. The apostle had received insights from God that made him especially sympathetic to Gentiles. And he was a bold orator.

Paul felt assured of his central purpose—in spite of the fact that his ministry didn't unfold easily. He was constantly harassed by Jewish extremists, endured persecution, beatings, shipwreck, and imprisonment. If Paul had looked solely to circumstances for guidance he would never have preached a sermon. An abundance of apparent "signs" would have said, "Stop, go back. This is not the work for you." But because Paul understood his calling well, and had solid reasons for it, he was able to overcome these obstacles and continue his ministry.

Having a central goal helps greatly in decision making. Impulsive rabbits need a purpose in order to concentrate their scattered efforts in one direction. Cautious sloths need a purpose in order to get moving.

PRIORITIES

With God-given goals clearly in mind we move to the next step: *establishing priorities*. This brings us to the nuts and bolts of God's will. We seek to find out how, when, where, and with whom we can best fulfill our basic purpose. We must choose which of several options will best help us accomplish our goal.

A good amount of evaluating, weighing, and pondering is involved. But God has promised to work with us in this process. In the book of Romans, Paul urges, "Be transformed by the renewing of your mind" (12:2). God wants to guide us primarily by renewing our minds through His Word. That's the best way to get our priorities straight.

In November 1981, my wife and I were thinking of taking our two small children to see my family in the Midwest. A few weeks before Christmas the recession slammed into the film department where I worked and I was laid off. We had to call the folks and tell them we just didn't have the money to fly out. They were disappointed, of course. Dad was recovering from a stroke, and my grandmother had lost her husband. The more we thought about it, the more it seemed we were needed in Illinois. Should we try to go anyway?

We decided to ask God about it, but how should we pray? The one thing we most needed was a new job to open up before the departure date. So we took aim at that goal.

Shortly afterward my former boss told me he liked a script I'd written on youth and alcohol and said he wanted to pay me for it. When I got home with this great news, Kaz was waiting with a $400 check from Dad. These seemed to be nudges toward going to visit the family.

We were still not financially secure, and we had even given notice at our apartment—just in case. But concrete, relevant signs pointed toward us acting more like rabbits than sloths. So we went. And we survived. No debts, no falling behind. Squeaking by, but happily intact.

▼

INSTRUCTIVE SIGNS

Having a goal in life is beneficial; having priorities helps. But sometimes evaluation of a specific situation doesn't take us that far. What if we're faced with two or more options that appear equally good, or equally bad? It's not always possible to acquire enough information about alternatives.

In life's weightier decisions, the element of the unknown often creates our greatest anxieties. Take marriage, for example: No one is able to look down the road and see how things will turn out in twenty years. Heavy choices about our spouse or career usually impel us to scan the heavens for an arrow pointing the way. Though that's not necessarily a bad idea, signs, like roadside directions, are not all created equal.

Before Kaz and I married, when we were thinking about making our relationship permanent, we cast about for divine confirmation just like any other earnest couple in love facing the big decision. But the idea of trying to set God up to give us an arbitrary sign didn't sit right. We wanted the signs and the reasons to talk to each other, maybe even coincide. If we were to marry, then the quality of the relationship itself and its influence on other people ought to provide positive verification. Two factors stood out in our minds: We should be drawn closer to God as a result of being together; and we should be able to do more together than apart.

Lord, if you don't want me to go to the beach today,
don't let the car start.

Look for signs that make sense.

We'd already seen evidence of a mutually beneficial interaction. I'd shared with Kaz some biblical principles that had freed me from the legalism I'd inherited from my particular religious culture. This proved to be a turning point in her Christian life. Understanding her position in Christ and its relation to her experience as a believer cleared up a lot of fuzzy thinking and assured her that her salvation was not threatened by moral mistakes.

Kaz, in turn, had shared things from God's Word with me that elicited my respect. This was a woman who could enlighten me, not someone I would just pat on the head with a that-was-very-nice remark.

Having these positive experiences under our belt, we now looked for further evidence regarding the "fruits" of our relationship. One day I suggested, "Why don't we ask God for a concrete demonstration—Him blessing people through us? Let's pray that together we'll help someone in a way that we couldn't if we were apart."

A few days later a girl in one of our Bible classes asked us questions about salvation. She seemed quite troubled and confused. As Kaz translated, I began telling the girl about how we can know we are unconditionally accepted by God. As we progressed, Kaz did much more than put my words into Japanese. With her new understanding of justification by faith, she added her own enthusiastic insights, which helped the girl past her doubts. Kaz's excitement about assurance proved contagious. Our experience with this girl seemed to be a "concrete demonstration" of God's blessing. We had our first "sign with content," which was followed by others. The incidents accumulated: answers to prayer together, effective witnessing, mutual learning—these signs made sense.

Looking back from this distance, I realize that we had some blind spots like most people who are bobbing along on love's initial effervescence. But at least we carried a few good instruments with which to get our bearings. We knew we were headed in the right direction—fulfilling the requirements of a healthy relationship.

If you feel the need to ask for divine signs, look for signals that are in themselves a reason one way or the other. Too often we fling out something arbitrary: "Lord, let the phone ring six times at six o'clock," or "Make him miss his train tomorrow afternoon." These are essentially empty signals, without meaning, not evidence in themselves. But by aiming at signs that make sense, we make our prayers for guidance much more answerable.

Missionary James Gilmour, in the wilds of nineteenth-century Mongolia, found himself acting as a physician. Though not formally trained, he could usually do far more than the local medicos. One day he was called to treat two soldiers who had been wounded in an encounter with brigands. He dressed two bullet wounds without much difficulty, but the third injury involved a bone complication. Gilmour wrote in his diary: "I knew nothing of anatomy, had no books, absolutely nothing to consult—what could I do but pray?"

On the third morning a startling answer came to him while he was tending patients in the marketplace. "There tottered up to me through the crowd a *live skeleton*, the outline of nearly every bone quite distinct, covered only with yellow skin, which hung about in loose folds." This was a seventy-year-old man, wearing a pair of trousers and a loose garment thrown over his shoulders, who had come for cough medicine. "I was soon engaged fingering and studying the bone I had to set that afternoon." It seemed a rather comical process, but Gilmour was deeply grateful for the information gained: "It meant . . . I knew what to do with the wounded soldier's damaged bone; and in a short time his wound was in a fair way of healing."[1]

The best signs are the ones that enlighten, showing us things we can learn from. So we need to keep our eyes open. Someone intent on asking that God send guidance in one particular way—"Get me a medical book," or "Give me a revelation"—might have missed the unexpected lesson in anatomy that came coughing to the missionary. We need a habit of prayerful listening and reflection (the devotional life again) in order to see signs that make sense.

Being taught by God is one of the greatest privileges of the believer. And our Heavenly Teacher has more on His mind that simply the answer to a or b, Chicago or New York, Biola or Fuller. He wants to share "all the treasures of wisdom and knowledge" hidden in Christ (Colossians 2:3). Martin Luther said this of his habit of meditating on verses while he spoke with God: "I have often learned more in one prayer, than I could have got from much reading and composing." Instead of praying and then plopping our finger on a random text, seek to absorb the mind of God by meditating on many texts—the whole of God's Word. The best way to begin walking in step with the Father is to first sit at His feet as an attentive disciple.

CHAPTER ELEVEN

Prayer Turns into Life

ANATOLI LEVITIN, A Soviet writer and historian, spent years in the Siberian Gulag where petitionary prayer surely must have seemed frozen to the ground. But he came back quite spiritually fit. "The greatest miracle of all is prayer," he wrote. "I have only to turn mentally to God and at once I feel a force that pours into me from somewhere, into my soul, my whole being. What is it? Psychotherapy? No, it's not psychotherapy, for where would I, an insignificant old man and tired of life, get this strength which renews and saves me, elevating me above the earth? It comes from outside me—and there is no force in the world which could ever resist it."[1]

I've tried in this book to be as practical as possible about how to make our prayers more answerable; I've made a series of very specific suggestions about getting various kinds of answers. But that should not obscure the fact that all our prayers have only one essential answer: God Himself. If we are to discover prayer as a great miracle, as Anatoli Levitin did, then we must seek more than anything else the One who pours Himself into our whole being.

Our petitions are most answerable as a means to that end. I have a feeling that the most important secret of those prayer warriors who astound us with their stories of dramatic providence is that they were not really aiming at the stated target; they had their eye on something beyond. The greatest thrill of answered prayer isn't getting what we ask for, but seeing God in action. He becomes more real, more tangible and fluent, when our petitions and His responses intersect.

The people who are most successful in prayer don't just get to know God better in order to petition more accurately; they petition more accurately in order to know God better. That's the goal of this book: to help you pray in sync with the Father, so that you experience the joy of seeing Him act in response to petition, not just to increase your quantity of gifts.

While trying to communicate the Bible's portrayal of a personal God with my Japanese students, whose cultural and religious background permitted only the vaguest picture of the Supreme Being, I used a little experiment. Hanging a sheet in the classroom, I secretly placed an object behind it, blindfolded one of the students, and guided him toward the sheet as he extended one hand. Each volunteer got to touch the object through the sheet once and try to guess what it was—a guitar, lamp, or vase. Usually it took several "touches" to guess correctly. After a while we progressed to faces. Various students sat behind the sheet and their blindfolded friends attempted to get a feel for who it was, one "touch" at a time.

At the end of the class I explained that our exercise had illustrated a kind of praying. We can't see God on earth; there's a sensory barrier between us and the spirit world. But we can reach out to Him in prayer. And each answer to prayer is like one of those "touches" through the sheet, giving us information about what lies behind it. We learn a little more about God's character each time He responds.

HIMEJI, JAPAN—A LONG NIGHT IN 1976

Haruo leans forward, pressing his point home. "You wonder how I can believe in all this intangible religious stuff? Well, what if I told you there are private detectives and samurai battles, Hawaiian beaches and lovers' dialogues floating around in our room right now? You would find that hard to believe, too, wouldn't you?"

Seigi nods.

Haruo reaches over and turns on the television. "But it's true. I can't see the dots of color that float into this TV set, but I can tell by the results that something invisible is acting on the television.

"It's the same with God. He can be known by His actions. At first, I found the talk about angels and God's Spirit living in people pretty odd. But I've seen the results in people's lives."

Cut. That was great.

Haruo and Seigi were doing a good job of acting out the parts of a new Christian and his skeptical friend. They had become accustomed to the heat of 2500 watts and the purring of my Super-8 camera. Kazko, the Bible teacher who translated my script, was coaching the two young men well.

The film, called "Seedling," was no Hollywood production. I made do with a small budget, miscellaneous equipment, and asking, "Could you spare a few minutes?" But I was working hard to show that God is active and knowable. I was also hoping the experience would help solidify the faith of Haruo and Seigi, both new believers.

This was to be our last night of filming. The camera had to be returned to someone in another city the following day, so we were squeezing in the final retakes.

If only once I could set up a scene without being in a hurry. Makeshift movie making, it seems, always must be done on the fly with antsy volunteers. In college I had a phenomenally patient roommate who let me spend hours composing shots of him walking down the sidewalk. But now, when it really counts, the pressure never lets up.

One of Seigi's lines hadn't been recorded properly last week. So we set up a closeup shot. He sits behind a low table looking over the script. The lights are adjusted to lose his shadow on the wall. Camera and mike are ready. We roll.

Seigi does his isolated line naturally, but the camera sputters and skips. *Groan.* I check all the wires, battery light, batteries, switch, and lock. Everything seems okay. I shake the film cartridge.

Lights. Second take. Seigi is into his line, but the camera still rattles unevenly. *Please not now.* Just a few little pickup shots and the film will be done. Disgusted and desperate I take out the old batteries, which are working fine, and insert a new set into the camera grip.

Lights. Take three. The camera stutters again. "Okay," I tell Seigi, "let me roll about ten feet of film in case something is jammed in the cartridge." For some reason I put the old batteries back in.

Lights again, please. Take four. I squeeze the switch with great intensity and shoot a minute of film, willing it to clear. No go. The camera sputters on, doggedly erratic.

My head goes hot and blank. I stare at my little, black blankety-blank camera, completely flustered. There are no more switches or cables to fiddle with.

Then Kazko makes a suggestion: "Let's pray about it."

So the four of us kneel together, telling the Lord about our genuine need and put our trust in His abilities.

We finish praying and look at each other for a minute. I stare at the recalcitrant camera. There's nothing more anyone can do.

Take five. Action. The camera makes such a melodious purr in my ear that I can hardly hear Seigi's line. The chronic sputtering is gone. We're all shouting together, slapping each other on the back.

We shot without a hitch the rest of the evening and completed the film. I was anxious to see our last roll. As soon as the footage came back from the lab I projected Seigi's line. The picture frame jumped and skipped during the first four takes; the sound wandered out of sync. On the fifth take picture and sound were perfect.

I rushed to tell Haruo, Seigi, and Kazko. We celebrated a completed project—and also our glimpses of God's imma-

nence. Haruo and Seigi had heard plenty about the God of
Heaven, but they said they'd never experienced Him brush
by so close. He seemed to be projected up there, waving at
us on the fifth take—God close up, with His hands dirty, fid-
dling with camera parts.

Prayer is a miracle because it shows us what God is like.
In Himeji I caught a glimpse of a God involved in the nitty-
gritty of life, a caring Companion light years removed from
the image of some inscrutable, remote deity in the heavens.

Experiences like this encourage us to seek more of God
and to seek Him as a way of life. We find that to live is to pray.
Our greatest goal in life is to bring our whole being to interact with the whole of God. Whatever we do to make prayer
more answerable—aiming, setting up a rendezvous, taking
smaller steps, believing, persisting, confessing, tracking—all
these are ways to offer more of our present selves to more of
our surpassingly present God.

The renowned evangelist George Whitefield once met a
young country lad who presented him with a sack full of
apples as a token of gratitude for his preaching. The youth
had walked seven miles carrying the sack on his back. After
Whitefield had gotten to know him, he remarked wistfully,
"He has such a sense of the Divine Presence that he walks,
for the most part, with his hat off."

To exist is to seek the Father's presence. That's the testimony of the champions of answerable prayer. They express
their enthusiasm in various ways. Teresa of Avila wrote,
"Souls without prayer are like people whose bodies or limbs
are paralyzed: they possess feet and hands but they cannot
control them." Philipp Melanchthon's maxim was, "Trouble
impels me to prayer, and prayer drives away trouble." However
we describe its usefulness, petition matters most to prayer
warriors as the pursuit of the face of God; that's what gives
us the most sustaining energy in prayer.

Sometimes we have to keep reaching through that sheet
for a long time; sometimes it takes quite a few "touches"
before we make out anything distinct. But the nature of

our ultimate goal ennobles the whole process; we find the meaning to life in this stretching out. When I trace through my own past for signs of a purposeful history, the lines that speak most eloquently are always carved by prayer.

PUEBLA, MEXICO—A CHILDHOOD IN THE FIFTIES

So many other tastes have interposed and confused or diluted the memory of those special meals early in my life. But I can still picture our maid, Adela, rolling mashed potatoes in spicy tortillas beside the deep kitchen sink. She would quarter dewy mangoes, fry long thick banana slices, and stir the rice and beans together while I loitered by the stove, growing hungry, making mischief. I can still see her supple, bronze hands as they worked the cornmeal with stone mortar and pestle. At last she would bring the feast into the curtained dining room where my family smiled from dignified chairs.

Years later the realization of what a meek, gracious servant she was carries a sharp edge. But for her that humble state was invisible—like a fish's ocean stretching out infinitely, without comparison.

Other scenes linger vividly like something learned by heart. There was the time I thought I had been mercilessly abandoned. My parents and brothers had somehow vanished over the earth's edge down the street for an hour's epoch. I wept in terror on Adela's lap. And she, like a great painting animated only in the essential part, sat silent against the slow evening light from the window, gazing calmly into a great distance, stroking my head.

I suppose we always prayed for her, along with the missionaries around the world and Uncle Chet, who had something gloomy called cancer. We petitioned together, from the eldest down to me, once a week in the living room.

Adela had come from the mountains, from sturdy Indian stock, where folks are rooted in the soil for better or for worse and, ever barefoot, are shod by the very earth. In those green highlands life moves in rhythm and brims with labor.

One endless Sunday I grew ambitious. Why not teach Adela how to read and write? Somebody taught me. Adela protested, of course, but my naive enthusiasm prevailed. So she slowly sat down after watching me spread papers and notebook on the faded roses of our kitchen tablecloth. I printed out a few of the letters I'd learned not that long before, and she obligingly coaxed the pencil into crawling after them. I knew she could do it.

But soon, roller skates, marathon Monopoly, and reenacting World War II with my buddy Gabrielito swallowed up the teaching career. And Adela returned to her radio and solitary meditations.

Yes, we prayed. But she inhabited a place where only images carry weight. She'd been hemmed in by candled saints and offerings the street dogs devoured in secret. For her, Christ was a wooden figure, bleeding paint, carried above a drunken crowd on holy days. How could her thoughts ascend to Him?

The time came for my family to leave. My mother and Adela wept. I packed my best marbles and roller skated in the patio for the last time. Adela went back up into the village where the aged can still recognize most of life. And I discovered America. A new world of good and evil opened up: television, football, and frustrating females.

The family kept in touch. Adela sent a letter every Christmas. Down in the village square, where unclaimed animals and naked children mingle on the packed dirt, a white-shirted country gentleman always sat with his typewriter. Adela would go to him with her thoughts. Flourishing hands over the keys, he transformed the message into a flowery, formal proclamation. But, behind his effusive grammar, Adela's ageless heart was still decipherable.

The outline of Adela's features faded steadily as I passed through high school and college. Other faces and other lives captured my attention. But one link remained: prayer. Sometimes the link thinned into one old request among many others. But her name persisted as I sought the miracle we had left Mexico without. If only she could catch a glimpse of Christ.

I wondered how, though, up there in the mountains, with a clump of adobe walls and a well. No word on a page could touch her. How could the message I had heard men continually try to wrestle into our privileged heads ever reach, much less penetrate, her settling mind?

I kept wondering and praying, until one day I heard. The faithful Christmas letter came, and a couple of lines overtook me slowly. "I have become a Christian. In all my life I've never been so happy." The words sunk in and hit a nerve. Adela! All these years. How . . . who . . . ? I could only read again and again, "Christian . . . happy," and wonder.

Could it be that our ragged petitions somehow aid God Almighty in striking home that priceless blow of grace thousands of miles away? Come to think of it there's Uncle Chet, too. Once eaten up by the disease, almost gone, now growing old slowly, like everyone else.

After my hearty congratulations, Adela sent back the village typist's expressions signed in large letters by her own hand. She was sharing verses she'd read herself in the Bible! From the convoluted language these phrases leaped out like fireworks: "always a son to me . . . please pray for me . . . I have many great battles . . . speaking of our Lord to many . . . if we don't meet in this life . . . in Heaven."

Prayer turns into life as we make it more answerable. That's the goal of part 1 of this book: practical principles that can make it happen for you. Are you seeing new and exciting things take place as a result of your prayers? I hope the adventure is beginning. Remember the important ground we've covered.

First, languid, defensive prayers are exercised into shape. We pray step by step, focusing on solutions. We set up a rendezvous between God, ourselves, and a special need. Our prayers move out on the offense.

Then we make sure our basic spiritual gears are working. We remember to count whatever facts we have on hand as true. We make sure we're persisting in joy for a positive goal. And we check to see if any unconfessed sin is gumming up the works.

In the four previous chapters we learned healthy ways to exercise special kinds of prayer: how to ask the right God for the right thing; how to pray in harmony with other people; how to find our prayer gift by uncovering a pattern in answers to prayer; how to look for signs that make sense.

As you reflect on these strategies, you'll begin to sense how they fit together and reinforce each other. They build momentum and help turn prayer into the leading edge of our relationship with God.

PART TWO

Untying a Few Knots

As you make progress and further experiment with answerable petition, you tend to start asking more difficult questions about prayer. Developing a skill usually involves balance, perspective, fine points, nuances. It's the same with the art of prayer. These final chapters should help you refine your abilities.

At some point, for example, you'll begin to wonder about "impressions"; how far can you follow them in prayer? How do you know their source? You'll also question more intently the faith you need to exercise. Should you believe only that God is able to give you gift X, or must you also believe that you have received gift X?

You may question how answered prayer and God's sovereignty fit together, and wonder how sincere believers can go on asking the wrong God for the wrong thing for so long.

Part 2 is about untying these final knots that sometimes trip us up in prayer. These chapters should help us come full circle in our adventure through answerable petition. We started by listening more carefully to how God wants us to pray. We end by listening joyfully to our Father's illuminating answers as we "chronicle His grace."

CHAPTER TWELVE

A Space for Asking

God does not play dice.   —Albert Einstein

The captain is in his bunk, drinking bottled ditch-
water; and the crew is gambling in the forecastle. She
will strike and sink and split. Do you think the laws of
God will be suspended in favour of England because
you were born in it?   —George Bernard Shaw

The gods play games with men as [with toys].
                                         —Titus Maccius Platus

How can I believe in God when just last week I got my
tongue caught in the roller of an electric typewriter?
                                                  —Woody Allen

Whether you are pondering the physics of the cosmos, a Brit-
ish sea vessel's demise, fate in ancient Greece, or mishaps
in Manhattan, life often seems to leave little room for God's
benevolent providence. In fact, most models of the universe
that our contemporaries have inherited in principle rule out

prayer altogether. A world in which God is completely absent or one in which God is completely in control can both portend bad news for the petitioner.

In this chapter we'll look at some basic objections to the very idea of answered prayer. There are theological and philosophical points of view—some complex, some very straightforward—that seem to make human petition and divine response impossible or absurd.

GOD ABSENT

First, the more secular challenge. An old argument of the deists still lurks around as supporting suspicion for those who are inclined to speculate at a distance about, rather than come boldly before, the throne of grace. If the Ruler of the universe, this reasoning goes, places Himself at the beck and call of every human whim sent up as petition, then He becomes a fickle god presiding over a chaotic world, rather than the Upholder of a law-abiding cosmos. In this view, the more orderly and predictable the universe is, the less room there is for prayer.

This objection has its roots in the seventeenth-century debate about whether miracles are possible or not and summons up an antiquated, fixed, mechanical picture of the universe—something that everything from quantum theory to predictions about who will win the Superbowl argues against. In spite of being continually reminded by the leading scientists in various fields about how little we know compared to all there is to know, people find it hard to resist the temptation to absolutize the laws of nature that have been discovered so far and declare everything occurring outside those laws to be heresy. But we will probably never know enough to say that X event can't possibly happen.

The deist objection also implicitly assumes that every time a child kneels down beside his bed to pray, he asks for water to run uphill or an animal to speak English. If that were the case, and the Almighty acquiesced to every request, then one could certainly imagine a god scurrying around to upset everything Newton, Einstein, and Crick worked so hard to make us sure of. In fact, the great majority of petitions don't pose the slightest threat to physics, chemistry, or biology. And God is not obligated to answer every human request—or any of them.

People typically pray for good grades in school, improved relationships, business deals to go through; they ask that things go better. God can arrange circumstances so that good things will happen without suspending the law of gravity or amending the latest bulletin in *Scientific American.*

The mechanistic worldview really insists that God cannot be an active player in the world; the Spirit must be removed from the machine so that it can better be regarded in "purely scientific" terms. People haven't been able to put Him in any standard equation and find a verifiable, repeatable sum. Because God can't be quantified, He's not there—that's their bottom line.

The counterpoint to such a point of view is this: Because God is the Creator He must be there. How can we possibly rule out His involvement in the organism He fashioned? That would be like saying it's impossible for the engineer who designed an automobile ever to drive it.

GOD IN CONTROL

The second philosophical objection to answered prayer sounds more religious. It arises from a certain model of God's sovereignty. The argument goes like this: If God is indeed sovereign—having ultimate control over everything that has happened, is happening, and will happen—then how can our prayers possibly change anything? If God has a will about human events, and His divine will always prevails, then what do our individual desires matter?

There's also the matter of God's absolute, unchanging character. He's perfect; we can't make Him one iota more gracious or generous or more sensitive to our needs. We can't persuade Him to do something better than what He intended. In other words, we can't change God Himself, so why try to talk Him into something? What, then, is the point of prayer?

The main counterpoint to this open-and-shut case against prayer is the cluster of admonitions in God's Word that all but demand that we petition, that we ask God to act. We must acknowledge that these are the pleadings of the perfect Sovereign who holds all things in the palm of His hand. This is His will: that we ask. And He has promised explicitly to act in response to our petitions.

God desires real relationships. That should be obvious from both the passion and the theology of the New Testament. He doesn't just play pretend, with all His creatures bowing or obeying on cue, as He pulls the strings. God longs to interact with and respond to beings created in His image. Think of these great Old Testament accounts: Abraham negotiating the fate of Sodom with his Lord the dinner guest, Jacob wrestling with the angel of the Lord until he receives the blessing, Moses beseeching Jehovah to forgive recalcitrant Israel one more time. Above all else, these stories speak of divine responsiveness.

The old model of God as watchmaker, who did His job so well that He must sit back and just watch the whole thing tick, doesn't make much sense. Neither does a rigid sovereignty-predestination perspective in which God is so sovereign that He cannot respond to the cries of His children. The Watchmaker, of course, can do anything He wants with His timepiece. And the absolute Father can make events dependent on the behavior of human beings if He so chooses. As Karl Barth put it, "The fact that God yields to man's petitions, changing his intentions in response to man's prayer, is not a sign of weakness. He himself, in the glory of his majesty and power, has so willed it."

In the great scheme of things, God has created a space in which human petition can make things happen. That's His

sovereign choice: to invest human petition with that potential. From the earnestness with which Jesus urges His followers to ask, one could even imagine there is some divine
need for our petitions.

Part of God's undeniable zeal in asking us to ask, pleading with us to pray, must be that He is committed to act in
large part in response to our petitions. On occasion He may
do something dramatic totally apart from us or in spite of
us; He may very well strike a blow of grace out of the clear
blue sky. But typically God works through human beings.
In the great war between the forces of light and darkness in
this world, we have a strategic part to play. God could have,
through the agency of angels, presented the gospel to every
living man, woman, and child with supernatural vividness
long, long ago if He did not have some irreplaceable role for us
to play in His great drama of salvation. Obviously He wants
our involvement; He wants us to extend His power and influence in the world. From this perspective, our prayers are just
one more way in which we act on God's behalf; they extend
His influence just as our verbal witness or example does.

Does prayer change God's will? Yes, in the sense that
God is able to do more through our petitions than He would
otherwise. Just remember: That's the way He planned for
things to work in the first place.

CHAPTER THIRTEEN

You Have Received

IN CHAPTER 4, "Faith Enough," I presented evidence that healthy biblical faith concentrates primarily on God's ability. We focus on what our Lord can do. However, certain Bible passages suggest that we believe something in addition to that. The occasion when the fig tree suddenly withered before the wide eyes of the disciples inspired Jesus to tell them that faith the size of a mustard seed could move mountains. The Master also made this statement: "Whatever you ask for in prayer, believe that you have received it, and it will be yours" (Mark 11:24). This explicit statement about what we are to believe in prayer pushes Jesus' other remarkable promises about believing and receiving even further into outrageousness.

This promise, more than any other, seems to lend support to that withering process of trying to generate faith: "I have to make myself think that it's already happened, that I have what I asked for."

FORMIDABLE MENTAL TASK

To get our bearings, let's think back to why we are asked to focus in faith primarily on God's ability. We want God to

153

become bigger than our problem. That's healthy, that's reasonable, that's belief. Now what if we relate this principle to the specific things we ask for? Jesus asks us to focus on the thing received. I believe He wants His solutions to become bigger than our problems. He wants us to look at His concrete answers more than at the concrete problem. This is simply an extension of His desire that we look at His ability.

It's possible to acknowledge God's ability to do and yet never apply it in a personal way. We can count as true this great power in the heavens and yet not see it employed on our behalf.

Remember Jesus' exact words: "Believe that you have received it." What kind of things can we believe that we have as we ask? What type of petition lends itself to this affirmation? Forgiveness comes to mind. If I've sinned and claim God's pardon, I should certainly believe that I have received it. God promises to cleanse us from all unrighteousness when we confess. Or think of biblical promises related to the Holy Spirit's activity. If we ask for the Holy Spirit to fill us, shouldn't we believe we have received that? Similarly, if we need love for someone and ask God to give us His love, shouldn't we believe we have received it and act accordingly?

These certainly are healthy ways of believing that we have received. The best way to apply this promise is to something God has promised to do inside us right now. God wants us to do more than acknowledge that He is a great Forgiver. He wants us to affirm the fact that He personally wipes out our transgressions right now: "I've got it." God wants us to do more than acknowledge that there is this Holy Spirit around who can do wonderful things. He desires that we count as true the Holy Spirit's activity in us right now.

God's immediate, internal activities are the most appropriate facts to count as true in the sense of believing that we have received. But we can't shut the door on exercising such faith for other types of requests. Remember the context of Jesus' most outrageous promise. He had just made a fig tree wither as a sign of the fate of an unrepentant generation. Something external and physical happened. And Christ told the disciples, "Believe you've received and you've got it."

Now surely this stretches faith beyond the bounds of credibility. I can't imagine standing in front of a tree, commanding it to shrivel, and believing that it's going to happen as I speak. For that matter I can't imagine praying that a mountain will relocate and believing that I have that request, *presto*. Our definition of faith as something that draws conclusions on fairly obvious facts seems to go out the window.

But let's think about what facts the disciples had on hand at that moment. They had just seen a fig tree wither, as if in time-lapse photography, at Jesus' command. The physically impossible took place before their eyes. So, on the basis of that clear evidence, Jesus was simply asking them to believe that all things are possible—that was the point of His exposition. He wanted to widen the disciples' perspective concerning what could be accomplished in prayer. His image of the mountain, as we've seen, served as a contrast to mustard-seed faith. We miss the point if we get hung up on moving literal mountains. But if we had seen the fig tree shrivel on order, it would be quite reasonable to ask us to believe that all things are possible.

Christ did not make this promise about believing we've received to the multitudes. He made it to the twelve people who had the most evidence about God's miraculous power, and He made it at the moment when they'd seen one of His more overt physical miracles.

Faith counts as true whatever facts we have access to. If you have access to only a few facts, draw conclusions based on them. If you believe that God exists, but can't imagine a miracle taking place, then pray with a focus on God's ability. Invest your thoughts and praise in whatever you can conclude based on the existence of a Creator and Redeemer. You'll be surprised at how far your faith can stretch if you simply count as true the facts you have on hand.

But if you have witnessed God's intervention in your life

or in people around you, then you can believe more. You have a better idea of how God functions. If you've done good tracking, you may have established enough feedback to be able to believe that you have received—even when praying for direct intervention.

The monk Cuthbert of Lindisfarne must have had some experience of that kind. While ill he heard that others were praying for him and said to a servant, "What am I lying here for? God will certainly have heard the prayers of so many good men. Fetch me my shoes and stick!"

So don't be intimidated by outrageous promises. God simply wants to move us to count as true the evidence He has provided. Our problem is that we don't stretch our faith based on the facts on hand; we don't choose to focus on God's ability and on His promises. Instead, we get mesmerized by the problem. Typically, our faith lags several paces behind what God has shown us individually.

It's true that the evidence will rarely be overwhelming. We won't have an open-and-shut case for concluding that X can happen or Y is going to happen. Some room is always left for doubt. Faith is not the result of being pressed up against the wall by the facts. It often must pick them out of a lineup. But the evidence is sufficient. God gives us enough facts. We must choose to look at them.

Draw the conclusions, Jesus says. *Get off the ground floor of reality. There's more to life than yeast and dough. I'm here; I'm active. Start thinking about that. Take advantage of the obvious; push your faith as far as the facts will take it.*

Unfortunately, the idea of "having faith" suggests something quite different for most people today. It's often looked on as something of a consolation prize for the mind. When reason doesn't work or when intelligence weakens, well, then, try faith. Faith can become an excuse for sloppy thinking. Normally, if you believe something preposterous, which no data supports, you are called pigheaded. But if you declare that you have faith that something is true (anyway) then this pigheadedness is somehow sanctified. This kind of faith takes refuge in subjective ground. You can justify an idiotic notion by saying, "Well, it's a personal belief that I have." In this way one escapes having to articulate the idea clearly or defend it before others.

A little more on the mark, but not by much, is the concept that faith closes the gap between insufficient evidence and knowing. When the facts fall short, we can always stretch out faith as substitute evidence, filling in the gap and pulling us to a confident affirmation. This approach assumes there is an inverse relationship between faith and facts. The more supporting data one can accumulate, the less faith is required; the fewer the facts on hand, the more faith must spring to the rescue.

These pictures of belief contribute to the unhealthy experiences of those who think they can generate more faith. They must somehow close the gap between the scanty evidence around them for miracles and these great promises about all things being possible. Or they must become more naive, closing their eyes to what they know to be true and persuading themselves of other improbable assertions.

Jesus gives us a very different starting point for coming up with belief. The nucleus of faith is simply counting something as true, looking at obvious facts. We make our choices based on evidence, a little or a lot. It's a neutral nucleus. Just as choices can be good or bad, stupid or fortuitous, so faith can be good or bad, stupid or fortuitous. Faith in ice a foot thick is a good thing; faith in ice an inch thick is unfortunate. The object of faith is what determines its value. Jesus emphasized the value of faith so much because He is its ultimate and very active Object.

Shortly before Jesus' midnight arrest in Gethsemane, He told Peter He'd been praying "that your faith may not fail." Jesus also warned the disciple that he would deny his Lord that night. A few hours later Peter did just that. When questioned by suspicious strangers he said he'd never heard of this Jesus of Nazareth. At that point Peter's faith had failed. How? By not being trusting enough? By not stretching to believe the improbable? No, by denying an obvious and very important fact: knowledge of Jesus the accused. Under pressure, Peter had not affirmed that as true; his faith failed.

Our faith succeeds when we affirm whatever we do know about God. Usually that will involve expressing belief in what He can do. Sometimes certain experiences and explicit biblical promises will enable us to express belief in what He will do.

One important reason God wants to move us toward bold affirmation is that this helps us avoid getting into the wait-and-see rut. Several people I have known, who always struggled against the obstacle of unanswered prayer, seem to fall in this category. They are waiting for God to answer before they place wholehearted faith in Him; they're holding something back. And He never seems to come through—clearly enough. It's an unhealthy state to be in: making your faith conditional on God's present performance.

Admittedly, there's a fine line between this and having your faith grow in response to answered prayer. Our trust in God does widen and deepen the more we see Him in action. But sometimes we can't get that dynamic process going; we get caught in a standoff: Who's going to move first, us or God?

The factor that can get us off center, as I've said before, is exercising whatever faith we have versus not exercising whatever faith we don't have. We need to see that God has already moved a considerable distance; He's done countless things for us that we're hardly aware of. It's up to us to respond positively in some way. Instead of just waiting to see if God will meet our expectations, we can affirm something good about Him. That's the first step that leads us into a more dynamic world where mustard seeds move mountains.

CHAPTER FOURTEEN

Ears to Hear

DR. WILLIAM PARKER'S prayer experiment (which helped us understand how to pray to the right God for the right thing) resulted in dramatic answers, encounters with God the Father, and changed lives. But I found it almost as disturbing as it was enlightening. I continued to wonder why the people in the "random prayer group," who sincerely believed that prayer alone could make a difference, saw so few results. Specifically, why did they go on communicating with the Lord in such counterproductive ways? It's difficult for sincere Christians to believe that prayer by itself is not enough, that it must be combined with some psychological technique in order to be effective. It's almost like saying that God Himself is not enough.

Take Esther, for example. This devout, thirty-two-year-old schoolteacher, facing a nervous breakdown, was eager to prove what prayer can accomplish. At the start of the experiment, she told her interviewer that she couldn't stand her household, couldn't stand her school class, couldn't stand anything in her daily life. Esther felt that the presence of a divorced sister-in-law in her home was the chief source of her problems. She said that God alone could get the woman out of the house and that "prayer can give me the only possible mental and emotional help."

Further testing indicated to Dr. Parker that Esther was insecure, unwilling to make personal decisions, and rigid in her attempts to make her life and everyone else's conform exactly to formal patterns. While growing up, she had received little praise or encouragement from a strictly religious father who had been exacting, critical, and harsh in administering discipline.

Esther prayed for nine months, was tested again, and revealed no observable changes. The sister-in-law who seemed the focus of her problems had long since moved out, but Esther continued to feel that if other people would only shape up, her problems would disappear. She remained fixed on the idea that the world is evil and that real improvement lies in the hereafter, and so tended to accept depression and despondency in the present. Her physical condition had worsened, forcing her to abandon teaching and become less active in general. Most telling of all, it became evident that the God she was petitioning, like her earthly father, existed primarily to be feared as justly wrathful.

After I'd pondered this woman's experience, one question haunted me: If Esther had hang-ups that were interfering somehow with an answer to prayer, why didn't God Himself clear them up? If she was praying to a God she feared, why didn't the Father reveal something of His love to her directly? I had the same perplexity about Jerry, the young man we met in chapter 7 who saw himself as a misfit. If guilt and hostility were distorting his prayers, why didn't God point that out and nudge him toward more positive petition?

I couldn't find an answer to these questions until I related them to the spiritual life as a whole. From the perspective of growth in general, Esther and Jerry are not that different from other struggling believers: If Deacon Jones is such a good Christian, why does he keep losing his temper? If Sister Sanders attends worship services so regularly, why can't she stop gossiping?

Obviously God wants believers to deal successfully with habitual sin. But many apparently sincere, faithful church members don't. They keep struggling with the same old problems, year after year. So what's the catch?

When we see moral failures, few of us blame the Lord. We acknowledge that the Holy Spirit works to transform everyone, but the flesh is weak. God is always on the job, but we are apt to punch out too early.

It's the same with the development of healthy attitudes and perspectives. God was demonstrating His love to Esther and nudging Jerry toward more positive petition. But they didn't pick up the messages. The Lord puts it succinctly through the prophet Isaiah: "I spoke but you did not listen" (65:12). This is a refrain all the prophets echo. Scores of oracles are preceded by the plea, "Listen!" and followed by a lament on the people's inability to pay attention.

The divine voice isn't too reticent. Even when God was blazing in a pillar of fire, thundering over Sinai, and shaking the earth under Jericho, the people didn't really listen. Centuries later, Jesus observed the same tragic human problem that renders God's eloquent voice inaudible: "Though hearing, they do not hear or understand" (Matthew 13:13).

The Holy Spirit does at times break through our deeply rooted problems directly, one on one. We've all heard stories of transforming revelations. But apparently it's possible for us to block that divine activity—even while we are earnestly on our knees. We can avoid the solution, even when we're staring right at it. The idea that human beings hampered by the carnal nature can go on indefinitely in unhealthy, unanswerable prayer is frightening. But we have to consciously face it.

Most importantly, we have to acknowledge that our "personal relationship with the Lord" can sink into serious ruts. A strictly private religion carries many perils. We're apt, of course, to pray about everything except our blind spots. That's why we're encouraged to assemble, worship together, pray for each other, encourage and exhort one another.

When someone sees the light in a group setting, that's not something different from God's revelation; it's a pre-ordained part of it. God uses any and every means to get through to us.

At the beginning of Dr. Parker's experiment, one volunteer was pegged as Esther's psychological counterpart: Mrs. V, a wealthy woman whose physician had warned that she was on the edge of a nervous breakdown. She'd had three already. Mrs. V. had been married almost thirty years. Now that two of her children had married, she was finding her new role as mother-in-law trying beyond her resources. She told Dr. Parker, "I've been everywhere. I've tried everything . . . and I must find help. Maybe I don't look it, but I'm desperate."

Tests revealed a woman who repressed her natural gifts in order to conform to outward, sterile social customs. She wanted her children, her sex life, her position as a mother-in-law, all her relationships to conform stiffly to Emily Post or the "old school tie" or some other long-established code. Continually fearful of inadequacy, she was never quite sure she did the right thing in the eyes of others. Beneath her rigid attempts at control, a smoldering hostility waited to erupt.

Although worlds apart socially and economically, Esther and Mrs. V. both manifested the same profile: a rigid desire to conform, a tendency to blame others, and an inability to face reality or make decisions.

Mrs. V., however, was desperate enough to try prayer therapy. She joined a group and was confronted by the fact that her own insistence on conforming and keeping up with the Joneses had robbed her of flexibility and confidence. She had broken three times because she was so brittle.

Mrs. V. resisted this perspective for some time. Then, one day she was detailing to an acquaintance her weary preparations for a visit from her son and daughter-in-law. The man asked, with a twinkle in his eye, "Are you always that much trouble to yourself?"

This chance remark inspired what was perhaps the first

honest prayer of her life: "God, am I always that much trouble to myself? Am I always that much trouble to You?" She received an answer a bit later while looking through an inspirational book by Joseph Surin. The author wrote that there are so few saints in the world because so many people "give too big a place in life to indifferent things."

Mrs. V. began to see that God had made no two roses identical and that her personality and talents were divinely given. So why not make the most of them? As she continued in prayer therapy, Mrs. V. began to replace the stress and strain of conformity with a more joyful cooperation with God's plan for her life.

CHAPTER FIFTEEN

Following Impressions

KARL DE GRAAF, a dike builder in Holland and leader of a prayer group in which the members spent much of the time listening to the Lord, was once "instructed" to get in touch with a young, self-supporting missionary named Brother Andrew. Karl invited him to visit the prayer group. Shortly afterward he paid Andrew a surprise visit at his home.

"Hello, Andy," he said. "Do you know how to drive?"

"Drive?"

"An automobile."

"No, I don't," Andrew answered, quite bewildered.

Karl continued, "Last night in our prayers we had a word from the Lord about you. It's important for you to be able to drive."

"What on earth for? I'll never own a car."

Karl patiently explained that he was not arguing the logic of the case, just passing on the message.

A week later the dike builder dropped by and asked, "Have you been taking your driving lessons?"

Andrew, who didn't even own a bicycle, admitted that he hadn't. So Karl said, "I suppose I'm going to have to teach you myself. Hop in."

After a few weeks Andrew was walking around with a driver's license in his pocket—with absolutely no clue as to what he would ever do with it. But Karl beamed, "That's the excitement in obedience. Finding out later what God had in mind."

Neither man could have known Andrew would soon acquire a visa to enter Yugoslavia and begin his legendary trips through the Iron Curtain as "God's Smuggler." For years he brought loads of precious Bibles to isolated believers in his trusty blue Volkswagen— flashing that Dutch driver's license to officers throughout Eastern Europe and Russia.

Consider another incident. An earnest young man named Joseph thought he was on a roll. Selling Christian books door to door during the summer, he thought he was smack in the center of God's will, doing God's work. He was able to make some fruitful contact with a person responsive to the gospel almost every day. A boundless zeal propelled him out every morning to his difficult but rewarding task of pounding the streets.

One afternoon Joseph felt a strong impression to go back to an address he'd stopped by in the morning. No one had been home. God appeared to be urging him to return, and ever eager to be a part of communicating God's grace, Joseph responded. He walked all the way across town in the heat of the day, anticipating through his sweat what God had in store.

Arriving at the designated house, he knocked. No answer. He kept knocking; no one was home. Keenly disappointed, he walked off the porch and ran right into a feisty little mutt that had rushed around the corner, eager to protect the estate. Joseph managed to shake the dog off, but it tore his trousers in the process. Needless to say, Joseph didn't think much of "impressions" after that.

Some people follow spiritual impulses and seem to hit a bull's-eye every time; others propelled by impressions hit the bull—and fall flat on their backs. Is God sending mixed signals? Are some gifted in this area and others not? Some people certainly appear to have a knack for sensing God's prodding. Catherine Adorna, a pious fifteenth-century woman of Genoa, made it a habit in "special supplications" to wait quietly in prayer with a humble attitude for the Holy Spirit to move her to petition, as opposed to relying on her own "self-originating impulse." Her biographer Dr. Upham wrote, "When she prayed to God, under the influence of this specific divine operation, her faith could generally see the result in the petition itself."

In chapter 9, "Tracking Answers," we talked about growing in assurance about what we pray for—the topic of prayer. Here we're looking at how we pray, or more accurately, how we listen in prayer. What kind of certainties are possible as a result of "influences of the Holy Spirit"? Why do some people seem to get the signals wrong?

In thinking about Joseph and his disappointment, I came up with one answer. This young man had been educated in an environment of legalistic fanaticism. Traumas suffered as a child made him painfully sensitive to the push and pull of duty and guilt. At one point he insisted on praying through the night, night after night, week after week. Looking more pale and haggard every day, he asserted that he was spiritually refreshed—just as Jesus had been after His nights of supplication. Joseph's personality made him a sitting duck for extremes; he was not so much moved by the "spirit" as yanked around. By the time he began selling Christian books, he had mellowed to a certain extent, but still retained the same vulnerability.

I've concluded that the attempt of a person like this to be guided by impressions is an invitation to be yanked about again. Who knows what welter of impulses his sensitive conscience and refined sense of duty could have bombard him with? Perhaps on that summer afternoon God was shutting the door on this kind of "prayer by impression," making a clear statement through that belligerent mutt.

Another man, however, who found consistent success in praying and responding to "inner guidance," presents us with a contrast. Dr. Ejnar Lundby of Norway left a remarkable account of his adventures with God's directives in prayer. Once he was propelled unerringly into a certain prison to rescue a man convicted of treason and murder, though, as it turned out, no one in the world suspected the man was innocent. But Dr. Lundby, following rather distinct impressions, was guided to the right evidence, through the legal red tape, and on to help vindicate the man just before his scheduled execution.

Dr. Lundby came from a scientific background; he was disciplined in the ordered world of medicine. When he first heard about the idea of individual guidance, he was skeptical: "I felt that human desires could so easily be interpreted as God's guidance." But he opened himself to it through a program of devotional training: "As I saturated myself with Scripture and developed prayer periods of quiet listening for an inner voice, I began to receive nudgings and communications which I could not explain in terms of my scientific training." Being open to spiritual impressions, becoming more sensitive to the Spirit's voice, was precisely the added dimension his life needed. Dr. Lundby possessed a balanced, secure personality and an ability to deal rationally with impulses.

Just as we may specialize in different areas of prayer, so our personalities may be best suited to different kinds of prayer. You may, through the spiritual disciplines Dr. Lundby practiced, reliably tune in to the Spirit's voice. Or you may find that impressions lead you into chaos. I'd say, as a general rule, that the more impulsive you are to begin with, the less likely God is to guide you supernaturally in that way.

Keep a careful record of what you pray for, how you pray, noting circumstances and results. Be honest. Don't fudge on the results of your spiritual intimations. It's possible to reel in all kinds of stray events as "answers" to what we are impressed to pray for. Make your prayer clear; make the answer you expect clear. If something different happens, it doesn't mean God isn't listening; you can still learn something. But it is one indication that your spiritual impulses aren't accurate. If your impressions consistently shoot wide of the mark, then a different kind of prayer is in order—at least for now.

I believe that most of us have plenty of room to grow in this area of sensitivity to the Spirit. We can listen more carefully and pray more wisely. After all, we do share in the mind of Christ, our hearts can be enlightened, we can taste the riches of wisdom and knowledge through the Spirit. All this can move us toward certainty. Many of us will find that, on blessed occasions, some moving target freezes in our sights for a moment.

But we must always acknowledge that we are fallible human beings. Everything connected with us is subject to the distortions of our sinful nature—including "spiritual impulses," however dramatically they may come to us.

Even Cotton Mather, of "particular faith" fame, which I explained in chapter 9, ran into problems relying on impressions. Cotton and his father, Increase Mather, then president of Harvard, worked very hard to obtain a charter from England for the college. While the Assembly in New England was debating the matter, Cotton prayed earnestly and received a strong assurance confirming earlier experience with particular faith that his father would be carried to England "and that at this very Time there was occurring that which would one Day accomplish it." But soon he discovered that "at this very Time" governor Bellomont was vetoing the bill for the college. This left Cotton quite confused.

He continued praying with his father "about the accomplishment of the Particular Faith, which had seemed so often infused from Heaven into our minds." Again he felt impressed: "The Lord Will do it, my Father shall be carried into England."

When the matter came up later in the Assembly and seemed about to be defeated, Cotton pleaded with God once more. He again felt assured, saying, "He will do it, He will do it! . . . If an Angel from Heaven had spoken it articulately to me, the Communication would not have been more powerful and perceptible."

But it all came to nothing. Governor Bellomont went to

England instead. And then the General Assembly ousted Increase Mather from the Harvard presidency.

After so much earlier success with particular faith, Cotton was deeply shaken. Groping for some answer, he speculated that the angels who communicate "Particular Events" might be ignorant of future occurrences and thus able only to impress men with what might come to pass "in probability." But there were more disappointments ahead.

Cotton's wife, Abigail, grew seriously ill in 1702, and he agonized in prayer over her fate. After some time, he was assured that God would restore her. Abigail lingered for months and then: "At last, the black Day . . . The Desire of my Eyes is this Day to be taken from me."

In an agonized attempt to understand this "Miscarriage of a Particular Faith," Cotton thought that perhaps Abigail had prayed for release, at cross-purposes with him, and that her petitions had overruled his. Or, he thought, perhaps God allowed this as a warning against pride or self-deceit. He became more cautious, stating that our own strong desire for what we request may lead us to interpret a particular faith too literally, assuming that "the Thing must be done in just such or such a manner."

Years later when his daughter Elizabeth came down with measles, then a serious illness, Cotton experienced powerful mental impressions but refrained from regarding them as guarantees from Heaven. "Having been once buffeted in that Experience," he wrote, "I durst hardly anymore countenance it." Elizabeth died.

It is difficult to reconcile the confidence of Dr. Lundby with the disillusion of Cotton Mather. Both were devout believers. It's difficult even to reconcile Cotton's earlier remarkable answers to prayer with his later mixed signals. But perhaps that is only because we expect too much from those impulses.

Can impressions, under the right circumstances, lead us into much more answerable prayer? Certainly, the evidence is abundant. Are they infallible guides to what God wants to do?

No, nothing we experience will ever be error proof. We may get powerful impulses that seem to come directly from God. But those impressions must travel through our minds—minds that drift through all kinds of dispositions, sometimes conducive to the right prompting, sometimes creating detours to the Spirit. We are a varying mass of avenues, not a simple two-way street.

Another observation may help. Dr. Lundby seems to have majored in open-ended devotion and listening. As he prayed in this state of receptivity, God's distinct messages often arrived unexpectedly. Cotton Mather seems to have majored in pleading; he yearned for a certain answer about Harvard College or his wife's health. In that kind of intense, agonized atmosphere, fervent impressions are more easily self-generated.

All of us need to strike a balance between sensitivity to God's inner voice and sensitivity to common sense. We need to pray because of good reasons as well as strong impressions. Honest tracking will help you determine if you are erring on one side or the other.

Spiritual messages are not necessarily either on or off—you see blazing lights or stare at a blank wall. God can communicate through the whole of our mental and emotional processes. Sometimes He simply gives a good reason an extra nudge. Sometimes He helps us reflect on the good reasons behind an impression. Calm assurances can be as valuable as flaming arrows of conviction. An insight from a verse in the Psalms can combine with an analysis of our circumstances.

Using the spiritual disciplines that Dr. Lundby practiced trains our hearts and minds to feel and think more accurately. We open our whole selves, giving God more ways in which to communicate. In that state of devotion we will be ready for those times when He chooses to act dramatically.

CHAPTER SIXTEEN

A Chronicle of Grace

IN THE LAST few chapters I've tried to unravel a few of the knottier questions and problems that sometimes tie up our prayer life. We've talked about how human prayer and God's perfect will coexist, about what to best affirm in faith, about getting the message and sorting out impressions. It's important to find biblical answers that make sense and to create a balanced perspective on petition. But even more important is uncovering those answers in the texture of everyday life.

I'd like to suggest something we can do to enhance the listening side of prayer. It's quite possible, as we've seen, to pray at great length and still fail to get the desperately needed message. We've also seen that some impressions wonderfully enlighten, while others lead to a dead end.

Listening is obviously important. We began that process by tracking the results of our petitions, keeping a record of what happens as we pray. Now we can expand that record to include a wider listening, a response to all that God teaches us through the experience of living.

Keeping a personal journal is a way of relating our lives more completely to God and His Word. It comes alive when we use it to chronicle the grace that the Father shows us in manifold ways. The Bible itself is an exercise in documenting His gracious activity. Its authors urge us to do the same, to meditate on His deeds, and remember His wonders.

One of the most profitable ways we can use a personal journal is as a companion to Bible study. Most of us have had precious moments with Scripture when a promise or principle impressed us deeply. Maybe we see a familiar verse as if for the first time, and for a while its meaning shines clear. But in time, the intensity of our insight tends to weaken. Other things crowd out the memory.

By keeping a record of what God teaches us in His Word, we can relive those refreshing times of revelation. Once, while feeling quite discouraged about my same old struggle with the same old sins, I read about how the priest Jehoiada orchestrated a brilliant coup (2 Kings 11). That narrative inspired me to fight more effectively. I made this journal entry:

> It would be great to overcome as if in Jehoiada's palace plot: muster up all the priests in Jerusalem, surround the court with armed guards, seat Joash on the throne, and lead a great crowd in acclaiming him king. When unscrupulous Queen Athaliah rushes out to check on the noise, she is forced to throw in the towel.
>
> Don't just trudge out with your small shield and try to fend off the flesh, world, and Devil. Go out with a massive show of force. Stuff yourself with the Word until you are surrounded by God's promises, wonders, commands, and righteousness. Get on the offensive, with praise. Overwhelm the Devil, don't duel with him.

The very act of writing down an idea tends to reinforce what we've learned. Putting our insight into words focuses our thinking and crystallizes God's point. Also, planning to record something often stimulates us to make more discoveries. Instead of just settling for a vaguely uplifting time reading God's Word, we dig up truths of practical value.

In time, a journal can become the commentary of our lives on the precision of Scripture. As we gain experience in applying its principles and claiming its promises, the Word becomes flesh in a new, personal way. We see it come through for us.

I've sometimes used my journal to record the things that inspire my most heartfelt praise. The spirit of praise is worth cultivating and preserving. At times we may want to note the circumstances that moved us to an especially edifying time of prayer. By recording the circumstances surrounding these prayers we ensure that the riches of praise reverberate back to us later.

> I woke up to squint out my latticed window and find the sun broadly bared against a clear sky. It has been gray and rainy this month. But today the whole atmosphere made a clean break with the past. The sun was so graphic on my neighbor's foliage, I was impelled to praise the Lord for all the ways He's like our daystar.
>
> The sun archs over us at a sovereign ninety-three-million-mile distance—and yet, it's instantly here, filling everything. It's presence makes such an overwhelming difference. Think of a child lying alone in the dead of night, wondering how day could ever possibly come again. Then all of a sudden, the sun's rays drain the universe of dark and transform the world.
>
> Yes, it's good to be warmed by the glory of God in the face of Christ "shining like the sun in all its brilliance."

Personal journals are also a way to stop and think. They help us reflect about where we've been and where we're going. Few things are more tragic than an unexamined life.

We build up a "listening ear" through our reactions to events we've recorded—what we feel and think. A little reflection often helps clarify our values, thus softening some of life's blows. It can teach us the relative importance of a new sedan as compared to the laughter of our children, or remind us of how much we used to treasure moments of communication with our spouse.

Sometimes we discover great value in something easily overlooked. Take this example of a nearly empty church sprinkled with a few silver-haired ladies.

> The service had finally trickled to a close. I slouched lazily in a rear pew as the smattering of worshipers filed out. Several women seated by the aisle remained, bowing in the quiet. One elderly gentleman, seated by himself toward the front of the church, slowly rose from his pew. He fumbled for a huge book, thickened by Braille lettering, and slipped it under his arm.
>
> As the man began to make his way uncertainly toward the rear, one of the grandmothers reached out and clasped his hands tightly. They exchanged a few animated words. Then the next woman at the aisle held the gentleman's hand, and the next, each one beaming up to him a greeting. In this way they formed an unobtrusive escort, guiding his steps toward the rear of the building, giving him their human warmth as fellow pilgrims.
>
> I looked up, and the man's face transfixed me. Around sunken, glazed eyes, his features radiated an intense joy. The women's hands had broken through his isolation, and he exulted in the moment.

God wants to teach us through life itself. Often His meaning lies just below the surface. Or our everyday surroundings burst with His signs. Finding God's messages in unexpected places is a privilege.

> After suction fails, our doctor grabs these nasty looking forceps. Big claws they were. I cringe as he takes hold of our infant and pulls hard. Then suddenly,

swish, the baby is here, plopped down soft and warm on Kaz's belly. I try to keep my camera and eyes going at the same time, don't want to miss anything. Non-chalantly, nervously, I check nose, mouth, fingers, feet—all there. A perfect firstborn son.

Then it struck me. Could Christ have been like this? God Almighty smudged with dark blood, squinting in the strangeness, head distended, limbs unwieldy as crowbars. For the first time I see the Incarnation.

His Father had to stand and wait too, taking a back seat to donkeys and shepherds. The One whose hands had not lost their skill since fashioning the orchids and gazelles of this planet had to be hidden, disarmed. It was a potent love welling up in Jehovah that opened His hands and delivered the Infant into our calloused ones.

All of us have moments when God's grace comes near. A journal is a way of absorbing those moments more carefully and turning them into positive memories. God does want us to get the message; He does want us to be moved by His voice. By listening creatively we can stretch our thoughts toward true wisdom, multiply our thanksgiving, fire our faith, incite heartfelt praise, and build a spiritual sensitivity to all of life.

Using Scripture to Improve Our Aim

Too often believers approach the "conditions of answered prayer" as simply a yes/no formula. We do certain things, pull the appropriate levers, and answers are supposed to come. Or we fail to pull the right levers and petition stops dead in its tracks.

It's far better to see these "conditions" as guidelines for developing a skill, ways to steadily improve our aim. God wants us to keep growing in our ability to hit a bull's-eye—more and more able to synchronize with His will and petition for what He is eager to do. And we get in that groove primarily by tapping into the riches of His Word.

Our Father has given us more than enough arrows that will fly straight and true: the precepts and promises of Scripture. As we've seen, Bible promises don't guarantee that we will receive precisely what we ask for every time we ask. But they do help us focus our petitions more accurately. The principles and promises of Scripture are ways to take better aim in prayer. And when our aim improves, our prayers will begin unleashing God's power and unlocking Heaven's storehouse.

In this appendix you'll discover key Scripture texts that greatly enhance the four essential components of healthy, successful prayer: *praise, thanksgiving, intercession,* and *petition.* It's essential that our prayer life involve looking as well as asking. Thoughtfully and prayerfully consider which specific verses can help you expand your skills in each area.

POWERFUL PRAISE

PRAISE GOD THE ALMIGHTY FOR HIS . . .

CREATIVE POWER—Isaiah 44:24
SUSTAINING POWER—Isaiah 40:26
SOVEREIGN POWER—Psalm 89:9, 97:5
RESCUING POWER—Psalm 40:2
VICTORIOUS POWER—Zephaniah 3:17, NASB
PROTECTIVE POWER—Psalm 18:2
UNMATCHED POWER—Deuteronomy 3:24
UNBOUNDED POWER—2 Chronicles 2:6, Jeremiah 23:24

PRAISE THE ETERNAL GOD BECAUSE . . .

HE IS FAITHFUL THROUGH THE YEARS—Isaiah 46:3-4
HIS NAME LIVES FOREVER—Psalm 135:13
HE'S ALWAYS RELIABLE—Genesis 28:15
HIS PROMISES NEVER FAIL—Joshua 23:14
HIS ARMS ARE EVERLASTING—Deuteronomy 33:27
HIS WORD STANDS FOREVER—Isaiah 40:8
HIS RIGHTEOUSNESS ENDURES—Psalm 111:3

PRAISE THE ALL-WISE GOD WHO . . .

SEES DEEP WITHIN—1 Chronicles 28:9
SEES FAR AHEAD—Isaiah 46:10
SEES EVERYTHING—Hebrews 4:13
IS PURE LIGHT—1 John 1:5
IS UNSEARCHABLE—Romans 11:33

PRAISE GOD, PERFECTLY RIGHTEOUS . . .

BIG AS THE MOUNTAINS—Psalm 36:6

SOLID AS A ROCK—Deuteronomy 32:4
EVER READY—Psalm 48:10
INTENSELY HOLY—Revelation 4:8
PURE—Habakkuk 1:13

PRAISE GOD THE MERCIFUL . . .

INGENIUS—2 Samuel 14:14
FORGIVING—Nehemiah 9:17
LONG-LASTING—Psalm 30:5
ON OUR SIDE—Psalm 56:9, NASB

PRAISE TO GOD WHOSE LOVE IS . . .

DEEP AND WIDE—Psalm 103:11
GRACIOUS—Psalm 36:5, Joel 2:13
STEADFAST—Isaiah 54:10
BETTER THAN LIFE—Psalm 63:3
PRICELESS—Psalm 36:7
ABOUNDING—Psalm 86:5
COMPASSIONATE—Psalm 68:5-6

BECAUSE OF ALL THESE QUALITIES, PRAISE GOD FOR HIS GLORY . . .

RESPLENDENT—Psalm 76:4
DAZZLING—Revelation 4:3
SHINING—Revelation 1:16
BRILLIANT—Daniel 10:6, Mark 9:3

JOIN IN AN ANTHEM OF PRAISE WITH ALL OF NATURE . . .

THE HEAVENS—Psalm 19:1
SUNRISE, SUNSET—Psalm 65:8
THE STARS—Psalm 148:3
THE TREES—Psalm 96:12-13
THE MEADOWS—Psalm 65:13
THE RIVERS AND MOUNTAINS—Psalm 98:8-9
THE SEA—Psalm 96:11

THE HUMAN SOUL—Psalm 84:2, NASB
EVERY LIVING THING—Psalm 150:6

DYNAMIC THANKS

THANK GOD FOR SALVATION SO SECURE, BECAUSE OF . . .

GOD'S CHOICE—Ephesians 1:4
HIS LAVISH GRACE—Ephesians 1:7-8
COMPLETE FORGIVENESS—1 John 1:9
AN ABLE ADVOCATE—1 John 2:1
SCRIPTURE'S ASSURANCE—1 John 5:13
CONFIDENT ACCESS—Hebrews 4:16

THANK GOD FOR WONDERFUL TRANSFORMATION WE SHARE IN . . .

LIVING WATER—John 7:38, NASB
A NEW CREATION—2 Corinthians 5:17
THE DIVINE NATURE—2 Peter 1:4

THANK GOD FOR WHAT HE SAYS WE ARE . . .

FIRSTFRUITS—James 1:18
GOOD WORKMANSHIP—Ephesians 2:10
SONS OF LIGHT—1 Thessalonians 5:5
HEIRS WITH ABRAHAM—Galatians 3:29
CHILDREN OF GOD—1 John 3:1
HOLY DWELLING—Ephesians 2:22
FRAGRANCE OF CHRIST—2 Corinthians 2:14
SALT, LIGHT—Matthew 5:13-14

THANK GOD WE CAN OVERCOME, BECAUSE . . .

CHRIST IS GREATER—1 John 4:4
WE ARE BORN OF GOD—1 John 5:4
GOD HOLDS US UP—Psalm 37:23-24
WE ARE PROTECTED—2 Thessalonians 3:3
WE HAVE POTENT WEAPONS—2 Corinthians 10:4

WE HAVE COMPLETE ARMOR—Ephesians 6:11
GOD WILL COMPLETE HIS WORK—Philippians 1:6, 2 Timothy 4:18

THANK GOD FOR THE GIFT OF FAITH THAT IS . . .

AN EFFECTIVE SHIELD—Ephesians 6:16
STRONGER THAN THE WORLD—1 John 5:4
MIRACLE WORKING—Luke 17:6
BETTER THAN GOLD—1 Peter 1:7

THANK GOD FOR HIS INVALUABLE WORD, WHICH IS . . .

SUPREMELY USEFUL—2 Timothy 3:16
A POWERFUL WEAPON—Hebrews 4:12
A RICH PRESENCE—Colossians 3:16

THANK GOD WE HAVE A WONDERFUL TEACHER WHO INSTRUCTS US WITH . . .

AUTHORITY—Matthew 7:28-29
INSPIRATION—Luke 24:32
RADIANT COMMANDS—Psalm 19:8
FLAWLESS WORDS—Psalm 12:6
EVER PRESENT COUNSEL—Psalm 16:7
ENRICHMENT—1 Corinthians 1:5

THANK GOD FOR MEETING OUR BASIC NEEDS . . .

FOOD—Matthew 6:26
CLOTHING—Matthew 6:28,30
PROTECTION—Psalm 46:1-2
SECURITY—Psalm 36:7-8
EVERY GOOD THING—Psalm 84:11, NASB

THANK GOD FOR GIVING US LIMITLESS POSSIBILITIES . . .

BOUNDLESS RESOURCES—Romans 8:31-32
IMMEASURABLY MORE—Ephesians 3:20

LIMITLESS GROWTH—2 Corinthians 3:18, NASB
EVERY HEAVENLY BLESSING—Ephesians 1:3

THANK GOD FOR A MARVELOUS HOPE IN THE FUTURE . . .

BODY TRANSFORMED—Philippians 3:20-21
TROUBLES OUTWEIGHED—2 Corinthians 4:17
HOPE GUARANTEED—2 Corinthians 1:21-22
GRACE DEMONSTRATED—Ephesians 2:7

SPECIFIC INTERCESSION

AS YOU PRAY FOR OTHERS TRUST IN . . .

GOD'S UNQUENCHABLE LOVE—Isaiah 49:15-16
CHRIST'S INTERCESSION—Isaiah 53:12
CHRIST'S DRAWING POWER—John 12:32
THE POWER OF THE GOSPEL—Romans 1:16
THE POWER OF HOLY SPIRIT—Acts 1:8

AS YOU PRAY FOR OTHERS PRAY WITH . . .

THANKFULNESS—1 Thessalonians 3:9
AFFECTION—Philippians 4:1
SUPPORT—Colossians 2:1
TIMELY WORDS—Ephesians 4:29, NASB
WORDS FOR EACH NEED—1 Thessalonians 5:14
POSITIVE REGARD—2 Corinthians 5:16-17
CONFIDENCE—2 Corinthians 7:4
ENCOURAGEMENT—Hebrews 3:13, 10:24
WARM RECOLLECTIONS—Hebrews 10:32

THE INTERCESSOR IS . . .

INVOLVED—1 Thessalonians 3:8
DEEPLY MOTIVATED—Philippians 1:8
NOT QUARRELSOME—2 Timothy 2:23
A GENTLE INSTRUCTOR—2 Timothy 2:25

PERSISTENT—Colossians 1:9
BLESSED—Job 42:10

PROMISES TO CLAIM FOR . . .

THE LOST—Luke 15:4
THOSE HELD CAPTIVE—Isaiah 49:25
THE HARDHEARTED—Ezekiel 11:19
THE INDIFFERENT—Isaiah 65:1, 1 Timothy 1:13
ALIENATED FAMILIES—Malachi 4:6
THE SICK—James 5:14

GREAT INTERCESSORS PRAYED FOR . . .

MERCY—Deuteronomy 9:26
FORGIVENESS—Exodus 32:32
RESTORATION—Daniel 9:17
STRENGTH—2 Thessalonians 2:16-17
STEADFAST FAITH—Luke 22:32
HOPE, INHERITANCE, POWER—Ephesians 1:18-19
GROWTH IN WHOLENESS—1 Thessalonians 5:23
FULFILLMENT—2 Thessalonians 1:11
OVERFLOWING HOPE—Romans 15:13
A SPIRIT OF UNITY—Romans 15:5
A HOME WITH JESUS—John 17:24

POSITIVE PETITION

AIM AT SECURE HUMILITY BASED ON . . .

JESUS, THE LOWLY LORD—John 13:3
GRACE—1 Timothy 1:12-13
INTERDEPENDENCE—1 Corinthians 12:22
LOVE—1 Corinthians 13:4
TRUST—James 4:10
INNOCENCE—Matthew 18:4
REVERENCE FOR CHRIST—Ephesians 5:21

THE POWER OF GOD—2 Corinthians 4:7
THE GREATNESS OF OUR LORD—John 3:30

AIM AT GODLY INITIATIVE . . .

DESIRE—John 4:34, NASB
SEEK—Matthew 7:7
DO IT WHOLEHEARTEDLY—Colossians 3:23
NURTURE YOUR GIFT—2 Timothy 1:6

AIM AT CHEERFUL GENEROSITY . . .

ABRAHAM'S HOSPITALITY—Genesis 18:7
MACEDONIAN WEALTH—2 Corinthians 8:2
EVERY PERSON'S NEED—Luke 3:11, NASB
OUTCASTS WELCOME—Luke 14:13-14
THE CUP'S FULL MEASURE—Luke 6:38

AIM AT RESILIENT PATIENCE, WHICH . . .

ENDURES—Colossians 3:12, AMP
REJOICES—1 Peter 4:12-13
BEARS WITH—Ephesians 4:2
LISTENS—James 1:19
HOPES—James 5:7-8

AIM AT JOYFULNESS . . .

MUSIC IN YOUR HEART—Ephesians 5:19-20
REJOICING (EVEN IN PRISON)—Philippians 4:4
CONTENTMENT—Philippians 4:12-13
THANKFULNESS—1 Thessalonians 5:16-18
ULTIMATE VICTORY—Hebrews 12:2

AIM AT PERSEVERANCE . . .

KEEPING THE FAITH—2 Timothy 4:7
REMAINING RESILIENT—2 Corinthians 4:8-9

SETTING YOUR HEART—Psalm 119:112
PRESSING STRAIGHT AHEAD—Philippians 3:14

AIM AT OPEN HEARTEDNESS . . .

SHARE YOUR JOY—Philippians 2:17-18, NASB
ADMIT YOUR WEAKNESS—James 5:16
SHOW YOUR EMPATHY—Psalm 20:5
ACCEPT YOUR BROTHER—Romans 15:7
SPEAK YOUR HEART—Ephesians 4:25

AIM AT SELF-CONTROL, WHICH IS . . .

INSPIRED BY JESUS—1 Peter 2:23
PRODUCED BY THE SPIRIT—Romans 8:9, Galatians 5:22
COMPELLED BY THE CROSS—Hebrews 12:4
TRAINED BY DISCIPLINE—Hebrews 12:11
SET APART FOR THE LORD—1 Corinthians 6:13
RULED BY PEACE—Colossians 3:15
FOCUSED ON CHRIST—Matthew 17:8, NASB

AIM AT SELFLESS LOVE, WHICH . . .

GIVES TO THE END—Luke 24:51
BECOMES VULNERABLE—Philemon 18-19
COMMITS ITSELF—2 Corinthians 7:3, NASB
COMES FROM THE HEART—1 Peter 1:22
EMPATHIZES—Hebrews 13:3
ADAPTS TO SAVE—1 Corinthians 9:22
CONSIDERS OTHERS' FEELINGS—Romans 14:15
OVERLOOKS FAULTS—1 Peter 4:8
FORGIVES AS GOD DOES—Ephesians 4:32
BINDS IT ALL TOGETHER—Colossians 3:14

Notes

Chapter Two—Setting up a Rendezvous

1. Judges 6:14; 1 Kings 19:5; Matthew 2:13; Acts 8:26, 12:7.
2. C. S. Lewis, *Letters to Malcolm, Chiefly on Prayer* (New York: Harcourt, Brace & World, Inc., 1964), pages 60-61.
3. John Pollock, *George Whitefield and the Great Awakening* (Sydney, Belleville: Lion Paperback, 1986), page 198.

Chapter Three—Defense Versus Offense

1. Ephesians 1:17, 6:18; Philippians 4:6; 1 Timothy 2:1-2; Hebrews 10:9-23.
2. Darlene Deibler Rose, *Evidence Not Seen* (San Francisco: Harper & Row, 1988).

Chapter Four—Faith Enough

1. Matthew 9:29, 15:28; Mark 10:52 (NASB); Luke 7:50, 8:50.
2. William W. Patton, *Prayer and Its Remarkable Answers* (Chicago: J.S. Goodman, 1876), pages 279-281.

Chapter Five—Praying Through

1. Steve Kemperman, *Lord of the Second Advent* (Ventura, CA: Regal Books, 1981), pages 136-137.
2. Ephesians 1:13, Philippians 1:4, Colossians 1:3.
3. William P. Parker and Elaine St. Johns, *Prayer Can Change Your Life* (Englewood Cliffs, NJ: Prentice-Hall, 1957), pages 128-129.
4. H. Clay Trumbull, *Illustrative Answers to Prayer* (New York: Revell, 1900), pages 99-103.
5. Andrew Murray, *With Christ in the School of Prayer* (New York: Revell, 1835), pages 35-36.

Chapter Six—Godly Momentum

1. Rosalind Goforth, *How I Know God Answers Prayer* (Philadelphia: Sunday School Times Co., 1921), pages 39-40.
2. C. S. Lewis, *Letters to Malcolm, Chiefly on Prayer* (New York: Harcourt, Brace & World, Inc., 1964), page 31.
3. D. W. Whittle, ed., *The Wonders of Prayer* (New York: Revell, 1885), pages 40-41.
4. James H. Smith, comp., *Our Faithful God* (London and Edinburgh: Marshall Brothers, 1914), page 125.
5. Smith, page 142.
6. William W. Patton, *Prayer and Its Remarkable Answers* (Chicago: J.S. Goodman, 1876), pages 181-182.

Chapter Seven—Asking the Right God for the Right Thing

1. William P. Parker and Elaine St. Johns, *Prayer Can Change Your Life* (Englewood Cliffs, NJ: Prentice-Hall, 1957).

Chapter Eight—Praying by the Numbers

1. Romans 15:30-32, 2 Corinthians 1:11 (NASB), Ephesians 6:19.

2. John T. Fairs, *The Book of Answered Prayer* (New York: Hodder and Stoughton, 1914), pages 292-293.
3. D. W. Whittle, ed., *The Wonders of Prayer* (New York: Revell, 1885), pages 28-29.

Chapter Nine—Tracking Answers
1. Kenneth Silverman, *The Life and Times of Cotton Mather* (New York: Harper & Row, 1984).
2. Elizabeth Elliot, *A Chance to Die* (Old Tappan, NJ: Revell, 1987).

Chapter Ten—When "Signs" Backfire
1. James H. Smith, comp., *Our Faithful God* (London and Edinburgh: Marshall Brothers, 1914), pages 146-147.

Chapter Eleven—Prayer Turns into Life
1. Anita Deyneka, "God in the Gulag," *Christianity Today*, August 9, 1985, page 30.